The Pocket
Small Business
Owner's Guide™ to
Working with the
Government

The Pocket
Small Business
Owner's Guide™ to
Working with the
Government

Marc Lamer

ALLWORTH PRESS
NEW YORK

Allworth Press books may be purchased in bulk at special discounts for sales promotion, corporate gifts, fund-raising, or educational purposes. Special editions can also be created to specifications. For details, contact the Special Sales Department, Allworth Press, 307 West 36th Street, 11th Floor, New York, NY 10018 or info@skyhorsepublishing.com.

15 14 13 12 11   5 4 3 2 1

Published by Allworth Press, an imprint of Skyhorse Publishing, Inc. 307 West 36th Street, 11th Floor, New York, NY 10018.

Allworth Press® is a registered trademark of Skyhorse Publishing, Inc.®, a Delaware corporation.

www.allworth.com

Cover design by Mary Belibasakis

Library of Congress Cataloging-in-Publication Data in available on file

ISBN: 978-1-62153-444-0

Ebook ISBN: 978-1-62153-448-8

Printed in the United States of America

Table of Contents

FOREWORD

So you've finally got your own small business and you're looking for customers. Why not consider selling to the federal government? It's almost certainly the largest purchaser of supplies and services in the world. While there are bound to be aggravations and annoyances in navigating the many requirements for doing business with the government, there is one huge plus: this is the only customer you'll ever have that you can be sure will never be filing for bankruptcy. It may occasionally take a while for you to get paid and you'll probably get frustrated at one time or another with payment delays, but if you deliver your product or service and it conforms to the requirements of your contract, you will get paid. So what do you need to do to be able to compete for, win, and perform contracts with the federal government?

This book is designed to give you a primer on doing business with the federal government. I will navigate the various and sometimes confusing legal and contractual requirements that can be difficult and discouraging for the novice. It is not meant to provide you with legal advice. There are many capable attorneys with particular expertise in the laws and regulations governing federal contracting. You would be well advised to locate one, for sooner or later you will find the assistance of such an attorney important to your continued success.

In this book I will use terminology that is regularly used in government contracting, but which is generally alien to normal commercial contracting. For example, when the government issues a contract following a competition, it is usually referred to as an "award." Responses to invitations for bids (IFBs) are "bids," while responses to requests for proposals (RFPs) are "proposals," or "offers." Concepts unique to federal contracting, such as "responsiveness" versus "responsibility," "discussions" versus "clarifications," and "price reasonableness" versus "price realism" will be explained in the chapters that deal with their subject matters.

There are many acronyms that are used in government contracting and I will be using many in this book, some occasionally and some more frequently. While I have tried to use the full terminology on the first occasion the term comes up in any given chapter, it might be beneficial to list some of them here. You may want to keep these handy for future reference as you may run across an acronym in connection with your government contracting that is not explained.

ACO—The Administrative Contracting Officer
ASBCA—The Armed Services Board of Contract Appeals
CBCA—The Civilian Board of Contract Appeals

CDA—The Contract Disputes Act

CICA—The Competition in Contracting Act

CFC—The U.S. Court of Federal Claims

COC—Certificate of Competency

COFC—The U.S. Court of Appeals for the Federal Circuit

COR—Contracting Officer's Representative

COTR—The Contracting Officer's Technical Representative

COTS—Commercially Available Off-the-Shelf

CPAF—Cost Plus Award Fee

CPARS—Contractor Performance Reporting Assessment System

CPFF—Cost Plus Fixed-Fee

CPIF—Cost Plus Incentive Fee

DFAR—Department of Defense FAR Supplement

DOD—The U.S. Department of Defense

EDWOSB—Economically Disadvantaged Woman-Owned Small Business

EPA—Economic Price Adjustment

FAR—The Federal Acquisition Regulation

FEDBIZOPS—The Federal Business Opportunities website

FFP—Firm, Fixed-Price

FOIA—The Freedom of Information Act

FPR—Final Proposal Revisions

FSS—Federal Supply Schedule

G&A—General and Administrative (expense or rate)

GAO—The Government Accountability Office

GSA—The U.S. General Services Administration

HUBZone—Historically Underutilized Business Zone

IDIQ—Indefinite Delivery/Indefinite Quantity
ITAR—International Traffic in Arms Regulations
LPTA—Lowest Price Technically Acceptable
NAFTA—North American Free Trade Agreement
NAICS—North American Industry Classification System
NASA—National Aeronautics and Space Administration
OFCP—Office of Federal Procurement Policy
PCO—The Procuring Contracting Officer
QAR—Quality Assurance Representative
REA—Request for Equitable Adjustment
SAM—System of Award Management
SAT—Simplified Acquisition Threshold
SBA—The U.S. Small Business Administration
SBA OHA—SBA's Office of Hearings and Appeals
SDVOSB—Service-Disabled Veteran-Owned Small Business
TAA—Trade Agreement Act
TINA—Truth in Negotiations Act
USML—United States Munitions List
VOSB—Veteran-Owned Small Business
VA—The U.S. Department of Veterans Affairs
WOSB—Woman-Owned Small Business

Chapter 1

GETTING STARTED

N ow that you've decided you want to compete for federal contracts, what do you have to do to be eligible? Perhaps equally important, what do you have to do to have a chance when you do compete? There are a number of steps you *must* take if you want to compete for a federal contract and a number you might *want* to take to enhance your chances of winning the competition.

REGISTRATION

Step one in competing for federal contracts is completing the registration process. In order to register, before a firm can bid on a federal contract, it must first have a "D-U-N-S" number. A D-U-N-S (Data Universal Numbering System) number is a nine digit number assigned by Dun & Bradstreet that is unique to a business. The service is free and it can be done online by visiting the D-U-N-S Request Service (www.dnb. com/get-a-duns-number.html).

Once a firm has its D-U-N-S number, step two is to register the business with the federal government. A bidder must be registered with the System of Award Management (SAM) in order to receive a federal contract. Go to SAM.gov to register. In registering with SAM as a potential bidder, you will complete various clauses and certifications that relate to its business. It would be a good idea to review these clauses and certifications before actually starting the registration process. It may sound trite, but it's always easier to get it right the first time than to try and fix the mistake later ("an ounce of prevention . . .").

NAICS Code

As part of the SAM registration, the firm will be asked to select the North American Industry Classification System (NAICS) code or codes that best describe the company's type of business. NAICS codes are a series of numbers maintained by the Census Bureau that describe virtually every type of business in the United States. Selection of the correct NAICS code or codes (contractors are not limited to only one NAICS code) is important because the Small Business Administration (SBA) assigns a size standard to each NAICS code. It is a firm's primary NAICS code and the associated size standard that determines whether it is a "small" business, and being a "small" business can qualify a firm for certain contracting advantages. It is the stated policy of the federal government to foster the growth of small businesses in the awarding of federal contracts. One prime example: federal law requires that, for most procurements, if it is expected that at least two qualified small businesses will submit bids or offers at reasonable prices, then the procurement must be conducted as a "small business set-aside," meaning only small businesses will be permitted to compete. Size standards tied to manufacturing NAICS codes are generally employee-based, meaning a firm's size is determined by the average number of employees it had over the previous fifty-two weeks back from the date of the determination. If the NAICS code is in a retail sales or service business, the firm's size is determined by average annual revenues over the previous three years. Determining the correct NAICS code is important because not all codes under manufacturing or service contracting have the same standards. For instance, while most codes for clothing manufacturers establish five hundred employees as the standard for qualifying as a small business, for shoe manufacturers the employee total is one thousand, or twice the total for other clothing manufacturers. As another example, for household appliance stores the size standard is $10 million in annual sales, while for electronics stores, it is $30 million.

It would be a good idea to study the NAICS codes before commencing the registration process, just as it was with the various clauses and certifications. The complete list of NAICS codes can be found on the United States Census Bureau's NAICS website. SBA's website (www.sba.gov) maintains the list of NAICS codes with their corresponding size standards. Always bear in mind that a firm's size is not permanent. A bidder may qualify as small when it initially registers with SAM; that does not mean it will always qualify as small. A small business will need to monitor its average number of employees or revenues as the case may be, for when it submits a bid or an offer on a procurement that is set aside for small businesses exclusively, it must certify that it is a small business at the time it submits the bid or offer. Falsely certifying status as a small business can have serious consequences. See Chapter 4 for more details.

Status Designations

As part of the registration process, a potential bidder will have the opportunity to designate its status for a number of government programs designed to benefit small businesses. There are, however, certain programs for which a company will need to submit an application and be certified for participation. In addition to designating itself as a small business, a business may designate itself as a Small Disadvantaged Business (SDB), a Woman-Owned Small Business (WOSB), Economically Disabled Woman-Owned Small Business (EDWOSB), a Veteran-Owned Small Business (VOSB), or a Service-Disabled Veteran-Owned Small Business (SDVOSB). To determine if a business qualifies to self-certify for one or more of these programs, go to SBA's website at www.sba.gov.

Among the programs that require certification by a government agency in order for a firm to participate, there is the SBA 8(a) Program for qualified minority-owned small businesses. Admission to the 8(a) Program will allow a firm to compete for certain contracts exclusively against other minority-owned small businesses participants. It may even allow a participant to receive certain contract awards without competition, up to a maximum value of $3 million for service contracts and $5 million for supply contracts. Assuming a participant continues to comply with the rules governing the 8(a) Program, it can participate for nine years before it must "graduate." The WOSB/EDWOSB Program operates in a manner similar to the 8(a) Program. A participant must be certified by SBA or a designated third party certifier in order to compete in a competition set aside for WOSBs or EDWOSBs.

Another beneficial program, but one which requires certification by the SBA, is the Historically Under-Utilized Business Zone or HUBZone Program. HUBZone businesses are small businesses located in areas (corresponding to census tracts) that have had a continuous record of high unemployment. Small businesses in those areas that meet certain eligibility requirements can compete in procurements set aside exclusively for HUBZone small businesses. Additionally, it is a requirement of federal law that HUBZone businesses competing in "unrestricted" procurements (procurements open to bidders of all sizes) receive a 10 percent price evaluation preference over their large business competitors. In other words, if a HUBZone bidder's price is within 10 percent of a large business's low price, the HUBZone business's price is considered to be the lower one, even though the HUBZone business would still receive that contract at the price it bid. See Chapter 4 for more details. To determine if a business is located in a HUBZone, go to www.sba.gov/hubzone and enter the address. The website will then show if the business is located in a HUBZone. There is no time limit for the HUBZone Program. A participant can remain a HUBZone business for as long as it remains small, its location remains in an area designated by the Census Bureau as a HUBZone, and it continues to meet the other eligibility requirements.

Finally, VOSB and SDVOSB contracting is worthy of a mention. While setting procurements aside for VOSBs or SDVOSBs is discretionary for most federal agencies, the

Department of Veterans Affairs (VA) is required to set aside a procurement exclusively for SDVOSBs if it is expected that at least two such businesses will submit qualified bids. However, while an offeror can self-certify as a SDVOSB or VOSB for set-aside competitions conducted by other government agencies (subject to review by SBA in the event of a challenge), in order to bid in a VA competition set aside for SDVOSBs or VOSBs, the offeror must be certified by the VA's Center for Veterans Enterprise (CVE). A good informational site is www.va.gov/osdbu/entrepreneur.

WHERE TO FIND OFFERS

Any procurement expected to exceed $2,500 (with certain exceptions set out in FAR 5.202) is publicized, at least initially (a reader may be directed to an individual agency's website for future developments), by way of a notice on the Federal Business Opportunity or FedBizOps website (www.fbo.gov). The site is set up with ninety-nine two-digit codes for the various types of supplies the federal government procures (with Code 99 being "Miscellaneous") and twenty-six letter codes for services (including lease or purchase of real property). The site allows potential bidders, by clicking "Find Opportunities" and then using the "Opportunities List" box, to search through all the opportunities (literally hundreds of postings each day) or, by using "Advanced Search," check those codes that relate to particular types of products or services. Be aware, though, the posting of an opportunity and the selection of the code under which the announcement will be posted is the function of a procurement official at the particular agency. I have seen some strange postings over the years, such as a recent posting by a Department of Veterans Affairs Medical Center announcing a procurement of "parking gates, barriers with installation training." That announcement, strangely, was posted under Code 84, "Clothing, individual equipment, and insignia." That is why it is always smart to check Code 99 ("Miscellaneous"). In my experience, when the posting person is unsure of which code to use, the announcement often gets posted under Code 99. Also, check any code that might remotely relate to your product or service. As an example, Code 70 covers "General purpose information technology equipment," while Code D covers "Information technology services, including telecommunication services." Yet, you are likely on occasion to see an information technology service competition posted under Code 70 or an information technology hardware competition posted under Code D.

Potential bidders should be sure to sign on as an "Interested Vendor" for any procurement announcement that interests them. There are often many substantive changes to solicitations (referred to as "amendments"; changes to contracts are called "modifications") or the due date for bids may be postponed. A potential bidder that has registered as an Interested Vendor will receive notices automatically instead of having to monitor the particular opportunity constantly. While it is not necessary in order to view opportunities, a potential bidder needs to register its business with the FedBizOps website and set up a password so that it can log in. Offerors need to log in to sign up for announcements regarding a particular procurement. Also, by logging in, a bidder can access the list of other businesses that have signed up as Interested Vendors who may be potential competitors or potential teaming partners.

GETTING TO KNOW THE AGENCY CONTRACTING PEOPLE

If you locate a particular government-procuring agency that makes regular purchases of your products or services, it may be worth paying that agency a visit. Pick a contracting officer from a FedBizOps announcement and contact that person. Tell him or her that you are new to government contracting, that you are interested in doing business with their agency, and would like to pay a visit. Most contracting people will welcome the contact, and while you are there you will have the opportunity to meet other contracting officers. None of this will get you a contract that you are not otherwise entitled to receive, but there will be issues that will arise from time to time necessitating that you deal with one or more of those individuals. Knowing the faces that go with the names can only enhance their cooperation. Indeed, our firm has clients who make it a point to visit their primary contracting agency on a regular basis.

Another source for potential contacts is an agency small-business event. Most agencies will have several such events during the course of a year, spread out throughout the country at the agency's various offices. Sometimes these events are geared toward specific small businesses such as veteran-owned or woman-owned, but mainly they are open to any small business interested in doing business with that agency.

In addition to agency representatives in attendance, there will usually be representatives of large business contractors looking for potential small businesses subcontractors in order to comply with their small business subcontracting plan. The announcements for these events are posted on FedBizOps, usually under Code 99, Miscellaneous.

DEALING WITH GOVERNMENT OFFICIALS

When dealing with government officials, bidders need always to keep in mind that many practices common in the commercial world are not allowed in the world of government contracting. There is a federal criminal statute, 18 U.S.C. § 1001, which makes it a criminal offense to make a false statement to a government official regarding any matter considered "material." While everyone is aware of the crime of perjury (lying under oath), it is just as much of a felony to make a false statement (or submit a false document) to a government official in connection with the performance of his duties, even though the statement may not have been made under oath. In addition to criminal penalties associated with making false statements to government officials, doing so in an effort to attain a government contract can have dire consequences. Under the False Claims Act (FCA), each and every invoice submitted during performance of a contract procured by the use of false statements is a separate violation punishable by a fine of not less than $5,500 and not more than $11,000. It does not matter that the government contracting officials knew the statements were false or that the government suffered no damages as a result of the statements, the subsequent submission of an invoice constitutes a violation—even if the invoice itself is perfectly proper.

Authority of Government Employees in Contract Awards

For a business electing to compete for federal contracts, there are some basic rules that are absolutely critical. First and foremost, unlike the commercial world, there is no "apparent authority" when it comes to government employees. If a government employee acts outside of the limits of his or her authority, the government is not bound by their actions. Thus, irrespective of whether a government employee's title would suggest certain authority, the burden is on the person dealing with that employee to verify that the employee has the authority to do whatever it is he or she is doing. This also means a bidder cannot rely on any advice given by a government employee unless the bidder verifies that the employee's position authorizes him or her to give advice.

The most common situation where authority comes into question is in the area of government contracts, both in the award and in the performance. For example, every contracting officer holds a "warrant," i.e., an authorization to enter into contracts that bind the government. However, there are different dollar levels to warrants. One contracting officer may have a $500,000 limit on contracting authority, while another might have $10,000,000 limit. Only a contracting officer with what is called a "warrant" can bind the government to a contract, and then only to the monetary limit of their warrant. A company may have a document that appears to be a contract, but unless it was signed by a contracting officer acting within the limit of his or her warrant, it does not have anything more than a piece of paper. A situation I was asked to review occurred a few years ago when a catering company was "hired" by a member of the Maryland National Guard (MNG) to provide meals to the MNG during its two-week summer camp at Fort Indiantown Gap, Pennsylvania. The company provided the meals for the two weeks and sent a bill to the MNG. The MNG responded that the person who hired the company was not an authorized contracting officer. The MNG informed the company that it was not responsible and that the bill should be sent to Fort Indiantown Gap for payment. Officials at Fort Indiantown Gap refused to pay the bill, since no one there had hired the firm. In the end the company was never paid. The person who hired the firm lacked contracting authority.

Want an even more outrageous example? In one well-known case, agents of the Immigration and Naturalization Service (INS) had intercepted a truckload of illegal aliens trying to cross the border from Mexico. Several of the aliens were injured in the chase, and the agents took the injured to the nearest hospital. The agents requested that the hospital treat the injured, and assured the hospital personnel that the federal government would be responsible for the bill. When the hospital sought payment, INS refused to pay on the ground that none of the agents was a contracting officer. The hospital sued the government, but in the end lost, because the agents who requested that the hospital treat the aliens lacked contracting authority.

While each contracting officer's warrant defines his or her contracting authority, there are certain actions that, by law, no government official can take. For example, no government official has the authority to enter into a contract in violation of the Anti-Deficiency Act (see Chapter 8). A contract that violates the Anti-Deficiency Act is unenforceable against the government.

Authority of Government Officials in Contract Performance

Performing on a government contract carries similar rules. Only a contracting officer can direct the contractor to do extra work or make changes in the work that it is doing. While most government agencies provide for on-site representatives to monitor contract performance, generally referred to as the Contracting Officer's Representative (COR) or Contracting Officer's Technical Representative (COTR), those representatives have no authority to make changes in the work. I cannot stress this strongly enough: If a COR or COTR (or any other government employee who is not a contracting officer) directs a contractor to do additional work or make changes, and the contractor follows those instructions without getting verification of the directive from the contracting officer, it likely will not get paid for that work.

Another thing to bear in mind in dealings with government employees is the presumption of good faith that they carry with them. Courts have routinely held that a government employee is presumed to carry out his or her duties properly and in good faith. For someone to prevail in a claim that a government employee was biased in dealing with them requires what the courts have said is "well nigh irrefragable" proof. Basically that means proof greater than a preponderance of the evidence and nearly rising to the level required in a criminal case (i.e., beyond a reasonable doubt). I often tell clients that if they want to pursue a claim based on the contracting officer having been biased against them, they had better have a witness who was in the room and heard the contracting officer promise to "get" that contractor. There is a corollary to this rule. If a government employee is shown to have acted in bad faith towards you, unlike the situation in the commercial world, the government (i.e., the employee's employer) is not responsible for any damages the employee may have caused you. That is because, by definition, a government employee who acted in bad faith was acting outside of his or her authority and the government is not responsible for the acts of an employee who is acting outside of their specific grant of authority.

Interpretation of Government Solicitations and Contracts

Government contracts are subject to the same basic rules as commercial contracts. In order for an agreement to constitute a binding contract, first and foremost there must be "consideration" flowing to each party. "Consideration" refers to the idea that each party must receive something from the other party, usually in the nature of mutual promises. Consider a simple example: Merchant Jones promises to purchase 100,000 pounds of Farmer Smith's tomatoes at one dollar per pound and Farmer Smith promises to sell the 100,000 pounds at one dollar per pound. Jones and Smith have formed a basic contract with their mutual promises, i.e., Jones promising the quantity he will purchase along with the price he will pay, and Smith promising to deliver that quantity of tomatoes at the agreed price. Now, contrast that example with this one: Merchant Jones promises to purchase whatever quantity of tomatoes he may choose to purchase at one dollar per pound and Farmer Smith promises to sell that quantity of tomatoes at one dollar per pound. In this example, there is no contract, due to a lack of consideration. While the farmer has committed to the price, the merchant has not actually committed to purchasing any tomatoes. Since there was no consideration for the farmer's promise of a one dollar per pound price, he is not bound by his promise. The same rule applies to government contracts. It does not matter if there is a one-hundred-page document with "Contract" written in bold sixteen-point type on every page. If consideration flowing both ways cannot be found in those one hundred pages, there is no contract. See Basic Purchase Agreements in Chapter 7 for a perfect example. It is also worth mentioning that there is no requirement that the consideration be equal or even fair to both parties. Consideration is sufficient if each party gets what they bargained for, and no rule of contract law protects a party from making a bad bargain.

There is another standard rule of contract interpretation, and in the case of government contracts it often works in the contractor's favor. It is a general rule of contract interpretation that contracts are "construed against the drafter," meaning that when there is any doubt as to the meaning of a contractual provision, it is to be interpreted against person who prepared the contract documents. Because the government is the drafter of all of its contract documents, it bears the responsibility for any errors or ambiguities in those documents. In the event of a dispute as to interpretation, so long as the language in the contract is capable of two "reasonable" interpretations (meaning that of the contractor and that of the government) the contractor's will prevail. The contractor's interpretation does not have to be as reasonable as the government's; it must merely be within the "zone of reasonableness." On the other hand, as with commercial contracts, words in government contracts are given their ordinary, everyday meaning. An interpretation that would twist the meaning of a word or a sentence can never create an ambiguity.

CONCLUSION

Federal contracting may seem a daunting task at first. If you take the time to familiarize yourself with the various government websites designed to help you find and compete for contracts, as well as those such as SBA's that explain programs designed to aid small businesses in garnering a fair share of the government's contracting dollars, you will have every opportunity for success. As important as it is to know how to find and win government contracts, it is equally important going in that you know the rules governing interpretation and performance of the contract you have won, for it gains you nothing to win a contract and then suffer a termination because you ran afoul of some rule or doctrine in carrying out your duties under it.

Chapter 2

GOVERNING LAWS AND REGULATIONS

I n government contracting you will encounter a number of laws and regulations. "Laws" are enactments of Congress signed by the president. While laws enacted by Congress form the basis for much of the principles governing contracts with the United States Government, most of those laws are too broad to provide the practical details for carrying out the policies embodied in them. It remains for agencies to issue ("promulgate" is the technical word) regulations designed to carry out Congress's intent. In nearly all cases, it is the regulation that provides the guidance for conducting procurements, rather than the original law. There are laws and regulations covering how the government goes about procuring goods and services, as well as laws and regulations governing how contractors are to go about providing the goods and services under their contracts. Some of the major ones are discussed in the following sections.

THE COMPETITION IN CONTRACTING ACT

The basic law mandating that the federal government procure services and supplies by way of competition (with certain delineated exceptions) is the Competition in Contracting Act (CICA), which became law in 1984. CICA requires that all contract actions expected to exceed $2,500 be publicized on the Federal Business Opportunity website (www.fbo.gov). The notice must be posted at least fifteen days before issuance of the solicitation, and the solicitation, except in emergency situations, must allow at least thirty days for responses.

Except for certain programs (small business set-asides, for example), CICA requires that "full and open" competition be the rule for all procurements. "Full and open" competition means businesses of all sizes are invited to compete and that any provisions in solicitations which restrict competition (such as geographical limitations) should be limited to those that are reasonably necessary to satisfy the agency's needs. Even in a set-aside competition, such as a small business set-aside, there is to be "full and open" competition among eligible firms. CICA allows for seven (7) exemptions to the requirement for "full and open" competition, such as where there is only one source, or where there is an "unusual and compelling urgency." When an agency seeks to utilize one of the seven exemptions, it must prepare a "Justification and Approval" (J&A) setting out all the reasons for the exemption, and the J&A must be signed by various agency personnel above the contracting officer level. The J&A must also be published on www.fbo.gov so that other potential sources can make themselves known to a contracting agency.

THE FEDERAL ACQUISITION REGULATION

The basic and most expansive of the procurement regulations is the Federal Acquisition Regulation, commonly known as the FAR. The FAR can be found in Title 48 of Code of Federal Regulations. It is huge, consisting of fifty (50) parts, most of which have multiple sub-parts. The title of a particular part shows what subjects are covered in that part (Part 15 covers "Contracting by Negotiation," for example). How it works, simply, is that the FAR will lay out a requirement, which will be found somewhere in Parts 1-51 (Parts 20, 21, and 40 are "reserved" at the moment). The particular FAR provision will then identify a standard FAR contractual clause, which is incorporated into a solicitation so as to make the regulation applicable to that solicitation. All clauses are set out in full in Part 52. Part 53 then depicts all the various official forms used in government contracting. The FAR is ever changing. New requirements and clauses are constantly being added, while others are deleted. Many of the changes in the FAR are designed to carry out executive orders from the president, such as when the second President Bush issued an executive order directing that federal contractors use the E-verify system to check on new employees' work status, or the one issued by President Obama requiring that successor contractors offer the predecessor contractor's employees the right to keep their jobs. Some clauses have remained the same since the FAR was first issued in 1984, while others have been revised many times since then.

It is important that bidders bear in mind that some FAR clauses are mandatory for all contracts, while others are mandatory if the contract is over a certain dollar amount. Still other clauses may be included at the discretion of contracting agency officials. The reason this is important is that clauses that are considered mandatory are deemed to be a part of all government contracts, even if contracting officials neglected to include them in the original solicitation. This is known as "The Christian Doctrine," after a 1963 Court of Claims decision in the case of *G.I. Christian & Assoc. v. United States*. The court ruled that a mandatory Congressional enactment must be read into a government contract, even where the clauses carrying out that enactment were omitted. Prime examples are the "Termination for Convenience of the Government" clause and the "Changes" clause. On the other hand, those FAR provisions that are discretionary are only part of a contract when the applicable clause has been included. The important thing to remember is that just because a clause is not included in a solicitation on which a bidder is bidding, it does not mean it will not be considered a part of the contract that is awarded.

Bidders should also keep in mind that not all federal contracts are covered by the FAR; only those contracts awarded by agencies of the Executive Branch are subject to the FAR, and even then only contracts for supplies and services. Contracts entered into by agents of Congress or the Courts are not subject to the FAR. Contracts that are not for supplies or services—concession contracts, for example—are not subject to the FAR. Contracts not subject to the FAR are governed solely by their own terms.

Finally, contracts entered into by federal procurement officials outside of the United States, while generally subject to the FAR, are not subject to all FAR provisions. A number of FAR requirements (such as certain small business programs) are not applicable to contracts awarded outside of the United States and its "outlying territories" (Puerto Rico, the Virgin Islands, and Guam are examples of "outlying territories"). Bidders competing for a contract being awarded by contracting officials located outside of the U.S. (such as an Army installation in Europe) will need to ascertain which FAR requirements are applicable and which are not. The solicitation should make that clear.

OTHER AGENCY PROCUREMENT REGULATIONS

Also, procurement agencies are authorized to have their own procurement regulations (referred to as FAR supplements). These regulations take standard FAR provisions and tailor them to the needs of the particular procuring agency. The most extensive of the FAR supplements is, as you might expect, the Department of Defense FAR Supplement (referred to usually as "the DFARs"). Therefore, bidders on a particular solicitation should be aware of the requirements of that contracting agency's FAR supplement insofar as they may impact on the resultant contract. Agency FAR supplements can also be found in Title 48 of the Code of Federal Acquisitions.

THE FREEDOM OF INFORMATION ACT

While not strictly speaking a procurement law or regulation, the Freedom of Information Act (FOIA) has become important in the area of federal contracts. When most government records became available to the public by way of FOIA requests, contract "abuses" like $400 toilet seats and $600 hammers made the nightly news. A potential government contractor can use the FOIA to its advantage. It can allow a firm to learn who the current contractors supplying an item or service are (know your competitors). A potential bidder can learn the price history of particular item on which it would like to bid. All federal agencies are required to have FOIA offices. For most it is the Public Affairs Office and there will likely be information on that office's website instructing you how to submit an FOIA request (and requests can generally be submitted online).

LABOR LAWS APPLICABLE TO GOVERNMENT CONTRACTORS

There are a number of laws covering government contractors that deal specifically with employment issues, any of which can have a significant impact on a firm's bidding strategy and the bottom line. Some are applicable to all employers, while some only apply if the firm is a government contractor. Generally, these laws, insofar as they are applicable to government contractors, are implemented by the FAR. The applicable FAR provisions can be found in Part 22, "Application of Labor Laws to Government Acquisitions." The following sections provide a brief recap of these laws.

Contract Work Hours and Safety Standards Act

This statute, implemented by FAR 22.300, requires that any mechanic or laborer working on a federal contract be paid at a rate of one and a half times basic pay for every hour worked in excess of forty hours in a week. Failure to pay the required overtime rate can subject the contractor to a fine of ten dollars per affected employee for each day overtime pay was due but not paid. These requirements are implemented by a clause at FAR 52.222-4. However, the clause is not to be included in certain contracts, including contracts where the value is expected to be under $150,000, contracts for commercial items, contracts to be performed outside the United States, or contracts otherwise covered by the Walsh-Healy Public Contracts Act.

Davis-Bacon Act

The Davis-Bacon Act (DBA) deals with wages and benefits that must be paid to all employees working on a government construction contract. The DBA covers all federally funded or assisted contracts over $2,000 for construction, alteration, or repair (including painting and decorating) of public buildings or public works. Offerors can find the applicable regulations in FAR 22.4.

Each solicitation for a construction contract will contain a table showing the Department of Labor (DOL) determination of the prevailing wage and benefit rates for each and every type of job expected to be required under the contract to be awarded. If an offeror receives the contract resulting from the competition, those specified rates then become a part of its contract and the contractor will be required to pay its various employees the identified wage rates. The contractor must also either provide each employee fringe benefits to a level equivalent to the specified fringe benefit rates or, generally at the employee's option, cash in that amount instead. The reason for the "cash" option is to allow employees who may be covered by a spouse's health insurance to forego his or her health insurance and take the equivalent cash instead.

In putting together a bid, it would be wise to use those prevailing wage and benefit rates in computing your expected labor costs. The DBA requires the prime contractor to keep certified records of payments to its employees and those records will be checked. Contractors with DBA covered contracts are also required to ensure that their subcontractors are paying prevailing wages and benefits to their employees. Failure to pay prevailing wages to employees or ensure that subcontractors pay prevailing wages and benefits to their employees can have disastrous consequences. The DOL can fine a contractor the amount of any underpayment, collect the fine, and distribute the money to the affected employees. A contractor can be suspended from all federal contracting for failure to pay prevailing wages, and certifying false payment records is potentially a felony under 18 U.S.C. § 1001.

Contractors have tried many schemes over the years to allow them to bid at prices that will avoid the payment of prevailing wages and benefits, to their employees. One often-used tactic in construction is subcontracting to a "partnership." Partners in a partnership are not paid "wages." They receive a draw against profits, and what the partners end up making for their labor is a share of the profits. Forget it. The prime contractor is responsible to ensure that all of the "partners" receive the appropriate compensation for each hour of labor. The "partnership" must certify that it has paid prevailing wages to the "partners" and the prime contractor must then certify it to the government.

Walsh-Healy Public Contracts Act

This act covers all government contracts for "supplies" (including materials, supplies, articles, and equipment) exceeding $15,000 to be performed in the United States, Puerto Rico, or the U.S. Virgin Islands, except contracts for commercial items and contracts for certain agricultural and dairy products. The Walsh-Healy Act establishes as a minimum wage the "prevailing wage" as determined by the Secretary of Labor and prohibits the employment of anyone under sixteen years old. It also prohibits the employment of convicts currently in prison, except under certain specified conditions. The act requires that employees on a government contract receive overtime pay for hours worked in excess of eight hours per day or forty hours per week. Finally, the act sets job health and safety standards. The applicable regulations can be found at FAR 22.6.

Fair Labor Standards Act

The Fair Labor Standards Act (FLSA) was passed in 1938. It currently mandates a maximum eight-hour workday and forty-hour workweek. It established the first federal minimum wage, required employers to pay time-and-a-half for overtime, and prohibited the employment of persons under eighteen in dangerous jobs and persons under sixteen during school hours. The FLSA applies to all employees or

companies engaged in interstate commerce or in the production of products for interstate commerce (unless an
exemption can be claimed). However, it does not apply to
"white collar employees," such as professional, administrative, or executive employees. Nor does it cover "independent
contractors."

Amendments to the FLSA include: the Contract Work
Hours and Safety Standards Act (1962) that combined all of
the many laws governing hours for laborers into a single statute; the Equal Pay Act (1963), banning discrimination in
wages based on sex ("equal pay for equal work"); and the Age
Discrimination in Employment Act (1967), prohibiting discrimination in employment against persons forty and older.
Also, a section of the Patient Protection and Affordable Care
Act (2010), often referred to as "Obamacare," amended the
FLSA to require that employers provide break time for nursing mothers to express milk and to make available "a place
other than a bathroom, that is shielded from view and free
from intrusion from coworkers and the public" for nursing
mothers to express milk.

Service Contract Act

Like the DBA, the Service Contract Act (SCA) deals with
wages and benefits that must be paid to employees working
on a government contract. The SCA is applicable to federal
service contracts performed in the United States and exceeding $2,500. In this instance, "service contract" refers to a
contract that is primarily one for services, as opposed to
a contract for supplies that may have a service component

(such as warehousing). It requires that prime contractors and subcontractors on such service contracts pay their employees in various classes no less than the wage rates and fringe benefit rates either identified as "prevailing" in the geographic area of contract performance by the DOL or contained in a predecessor contractor's union contract. The SCA is covered by regulations found in FAR 22.10.

The following examples illustrate some of the types of services that are considered to be covered by the SCA:

a. Motor pool operation, parking, taxicab, and ambulance services.

b. Packing, crating, and storage.

c. Custodial, janitorial, housekeeping, and guard services.

d. Food service and lodging.

e. Laundry, dry-cleaning, linen supply, and clothing alteration and repair services.

f. Snow, trash, and garbage removal.

g. Aerial spraying and aerial reconnaissance for fire detection.

h. Some support services at installations, including grounds maintenance and landscaping.

i. Certain specialized services requiring specific skills, such as drafting, illustrating, graphic arts, stenographic reporting, or mortuary services.

j. Electronic equipment maintenance and operation and engineering support services.

k. Maintenance and repair of all types of equipment, for example: aircraft, engines, electrical motors, vehicles, and electronic, office, and related business and construction equipment.

l. Operation, maintenance, or logistics support of a federal facility.

m. Data collection, processing, and analysis services.

In the case of the SCA, like the DBA, the solicitation will include a DOL wage determination for each job description that will be required in the resulting contract. The bidder awarded the contract will be required to pay its various employees the prevailing wages and fringe benefits (or the equivalent cash). Another SCA provision ensures that if the predecessor contractor's employees were covered by a collective bargaining agreement (meaning a union contract), then the new contractor must pay its employees working on the contract wages and fringe benefits at least equal to those called for in that union contract. The FAR requires that the contracting officer conducting the new competition determine if there is a union contract in place and use that union contract as the basis for the wage determinations to be included in the solicitation.

The SCA, as is the case with the DBA, requires that the prime contractor keep certified records of payments to its employees and those records, once again, will be checked. Likewise, prime contractors are required to ensure that their subcontractors are paying prevailing wages and benefits to their employees. A failure by the contractor to pay prevailing wages to its employees or ensure that its subcontractors pay prevailing wages and benefits to their employees is subject to the same sort of penalties as with the DBA. The DOL can fine the contractor an amount equal to any underpayment, collect the fine, and distribute the money to the affected employees. Upon request from the DOL, the contracting officer can withhold payments under the contract to provide a fund for payment of the amount of any underpayment to the affected employees. A contractor can be suspended from all federal contracting for failure to pay prevailing wages, and certifying false payment records is potentially a felony under 18 U.S.C. § 1001.

Americans with Disabilities Act

The Americans with Disabilities Act (the ADA), enacted in 1990, applies to all employers, not just government contractors. It protects individuals with disabilities (physical or mental) from being discriminated against and requires contractors to make "reasonable accommodation" for such an employee. Disability is defined by the ADA as ". . . a physical or mental impairment that substantially limits a major life activity." Essentially, it grants the same protection to persons with disabilities as the Civil Rights Act of 1964, which banned discrimination based on race, religion, sex, national origin, or certain other characteristics. The ADA is enforced by the Equal Employment Opportunity Commission (EEOC).

The Drug Free Work Place Act

The Drug Free Work Place Act (the DFWPA), which is implemented in FAR Subpart 23.5, prohibits the federal government from awarding a contract to a contractor unless it has certified that it will maintain a drug-free workplace. The DFWP does not require that a contractor subject its employees to drug testing. However, federal contractors are required to:

- Make a good faith effort to maintain a drug-free workplace.

- Establish and publish to employees a policy prohibiting unlawful drug-related activity in the workplace and specifying actions that will be taken in the event of a violation.

- Establish a drug-free awareness program, informing employees about the requirements for a drug-free workplace and the availability of counseling.

- Notify the government-contracting agency in writing of an employee's drug-related criminal conviction within ten calendar days after learning of it.

- Impose sanctions, up to and including termination of an employee involved in drug-related activity, or require the employee to participate in drug-abuse assistance or rehabilitation programs.

Non-Displacement of Qualified Workers

While this requirement stems from an executive order signed by President Obama in 2010 rather than a law, so long as it remains in effect it has the force and effect of law. This executive order requires an offeror that is successful in winning a service contract to offer the former contractor's service employees the opportunity to keep their jobs. The specifics of how this requirement is to be implemented and carried out can be found in the FAR clause at 52.222-17, "Nondisplacement of Qualified Workers," which is included in all solicitations for service contracts.

Employment Eligibility Verification (E-Verify)

While not actually a law, the Department of Homeland Security's (DHS) E-verify program is a significant employment-related program for government contractors. It is designed to ensure that in performing on a government contract, contractors employ only persons who are allowed to work in the U.S., meaning no undocumented aliens. There is an E-verify website maintained by DHS. By using the website, a contractor can quickly verify that a prospective or newly hired employee is eligible to work for it.

Under the terms of the FAR clause included in all solicitations, upon receiving its first contract with the applicable clause, the contractor will be required to register in the E-verify system and use it to verify that all employees performing direct and substantial work on the contract are eligible for employment. The contractor must also verify all newly hired employees, regardless of whether they are assigned to work on the federal contract. A federal contractor has the option of verifying all of its current employees rather than only those working on the federal contract. Since the clause is now in all federal contracts, the obligation on the part of contractors to check newly hired employees remains in effect so long as they continue to do business with the federal government.

CONCLUSION

No one can be expected to know all of the laws and regulations applicable to contracting with the government, but it can be important to know where to find the regulations relating to your contract and how to interpret them. For those laws and regulations that are particularly complex, there are attorneys who concentrate their practice in the area of government contracting and who make it a point to keep up-to-date on changes in those laws and regulations and how to navigate them. It would be smart to locate one that you can work with as needed.

Chapter 3

Contractor Ethics Requirements

I f you are going to do business with the federal government, it is important that you understand what you can and cannot do. In some cases, conduct that might seem normal in the commercial world can have serious consequence in government contracting. Here are some major examples and the consequences.

The Procurement Integrity Act

This statute covers conduct of both government officials and contractors. It has far-reaching provisions:

- It prohibits current and former government employees from disclosing contractor bid or proposal information or source selection information prior to award of a contract.

- It prohibits anyone (contractor and government personnel alike) from obtaining contractor bid or proposal information or source selection information.

- It requires that any federal employee who is participating "personally and substantially" in procurement contracts and is contacted by a bidder or offeror in that procurement regarding possible employment report that contact to the employee's supervisor and to the designated agency ethics official; the employee must then either reject the offer or remove himself or herself from further participation in the procurement.

- It mandates a one-year ban on any federal employee in the following seven positions on a contract of over $10 million from accepting compensation from a contractor. The seven positions are:

1. Procuring Contracting Officer

2. Source Selection Authority (SSA)

3. Member of the Source Selection Evaluation Board (SSEB)

4. Chief of a technical or financial evaluation team

5. Program Manager

6. Deputy Program Manager

7. Administrative Contract Officer

The one-year ban also applies to anyone who "personally makes" any of the following seven types of decisions:

1. Award of contract worth over $10 million

2. Award of a subcontract worth over $10 million

3. Award of a modification of a contract or subcontract worth over $10 million

4. Award of a task or delivery order worth over $10 million

5. Establishment of overhead or other rates applicable to a contract worth over $10 million

6. Approval of a contract payment or payments of over $10 million

7. Payment or settlement of a claim worth over $10 million

Distilling all of that down to what an offeror needs to avoid, it is offering a job to a government employee who is involved in a procurement in which the contractor is a competitor. While technically not illegal in and of itself, it can start a chain reaction of inquiries that no offeror needs.

There are severe penalties for violation of Procurement Integrity Act provisions. The clause at FAR 52.203-8, "Cancellation, Rescission, and Recovery of Funds for Illegal or Improper Activity," allows the government to rescind a contract in the event of a violation, and, in addition to the imposition of penalties, recover any amounts paid to the contractor. The clause at FAR 52.203-10, "Price or Fee Adjustment for Illegal or Improper Activity" allows the government, in lieu of rescinding the contract, to reduce the price (in the case of a firm, fixed-price contract) or the total cost and fee (in the case of a cost plus fixed fee contract) in the event of illegal activity. In the case of a firm, fixed-price contract, the reduction can be up to 10 percent of the initial contract price, or an amount determined to be to the contractor's profit.

COLLUSION IN BIDDING

One major taboo in government contracting is colluding with another bidder on the prices you and/or the other bidder will offer in a competition. This may take the form of an agreement between you and a competitor to take turns winning contracts, such as, "You submit the low bid on this one and I'll submit the low bid on the next one." Most solicitations in negotiated procurements include the clause at FAR 52.203-2, "Certificate of Independent Price Determination." This clause provides that by submitting and signing its offer, the offeror is certifying that it arrived at its offered price independently. As is the case with any other certification, falsely certifying that a price has been determined independently can be a criminal violation under 18 United States Code § 1001. Another form of collusion is the "courtesy" bid. Since the government is forbidden from awarding a contract at an unreasonably high price, contracting officers often determine the reasonableness of the low price by looking at competitors' prices. It is improper for a bidder to submit a high-priced bid on a contract that it does not really want in order to make a low bidder's price look reasonable.

It is worth noting that collusion in bidding is not only frowned upon in government contracting, it is also not permitted in the commercial world. Engaging in such activities with a firm's competitors can have both criminal and civil antitrust implications.

GRATUITIES

While giving a customer's purchasing agent a gratuity may be winked at in the commercial marketplace, it is strictly forbidden in doing business with the federal government. I am not talking about bribery here; paying a government official a bribe is a criminal offense. However, clause "Gratuities" at FAR 52.203-3 allows the government to terminate the contract if it is found that the contractor offered or gave a gratuity to a government official in connection with the award of a contract or seeking favorable treatment under a contract. A gratuity differs from a bribe in that a gratuity is generally more in the nature of a gift (entertainment, or the use of a summer house, for example), and unlike a bribe, there is no direct *quid pro quo*. A contract termination for violation of the "Gratuities" clause is considered a breach of contract, allowing the government to recover breach damages from the contractor. In addition, the government can recover a penalty of not less than three times nor more than ten times the amount of the gratuity. Finally, a contractor can be debarred for giving a gratuity (see below).

COVENANT AGAINST CONTINGENT FEES

It is improper for a bidder to promise or pay someone a contingent fee to assist in procuring a government contract unless that someone is a *bona fide* employee of the contractor or a commercial sales agency. In this case, *"bona fide"* means the employee or commercial agency is not holding himself or itself out as being able to obtain a government contract by way of "connections." The clause at FAR 52.203-5, "Covenant Against Contingent Fees," incorporated in all solicitations, includes a warranty that the bidder has not promised anyone an improper contingent fee in connection with award of the contract. In the event it is later discovered that contractor did pay someone a fee for using his or her influence to obtain the contract, the FAR clause allows the government to recover from the contractor the full amount of any improper contingent fee that the contractor paid.

BUYING-IN

FAR Subpart 3.5 prohibits, among "Other Improper Business Practices," the practice of "buying-in" in connection with a federal contract. "Buying-in" is defined as submitting an offer below anticipated performance costs with the expectation of either increasing the contract value after award by way of unnecessary or excessively priced change orders, or expecting to receive follow-up contracts at artificially high prices to recoup losses on the initial buy-in contract. Obviously, determining whether a contractor is "buying-in" versus submitting a very low bid to keep a factory working may not be easy to do. Because buying-in has the effect of decreasing competition, however, contracting officers are instructed to take appropriate steps to ensure that a contractor cannot recover performance losses through change orders or high-priced follow-up contracts.

Restricting a Subcontractor's Right to do Business with the Government

It is in the government's best interest to foster increased competition for government business. Toward that end, the clause at FAR 52.203-6, "Restrictions on Subcontractor Sales to the Government," included in all solicitations, states that the contractor will not require, as a condition for the award of a subcontract, that the subcontractor agree not to compete directly against the contractor for the government's business in the future. In fact, the clause requires the contractor to include the clause in any subcontracts the contractor may enter into, so that a subcontractor does not restrict its subcontractors.

Kickbacks

All solicitations include the clause at FAR 52.203-7, "Anti-Kickback Procedures." This clause, which implements the Anti-Kickback Act, prohibits any "kickbacks," defined as money, credit, gift, gratuity, thing of value, or compensation, offered to a prime contractor or to one of the prime contractor's employees to obtain a subcontract or favorable treatment under a subcontract. The government can offset the amount of any kickback a contractor or one of its employees received from a supplier or subcontractor against payments due under the prime contract. This is another clause that is mandatory for inclusion in any subcontracts the prime contractor may award, so that the same rules apply to subcontractors in their dealings with their subcontractors.

The obligation of a prime contractor though goes beyond simply including the appropriate clause in subcontracts. FAR 3.502(i)(1) requires that for contracts exceeding the Simplified Acquisition Threshold, the contractor have in place and follow reasonable procedures to detect kickback violations involving subcontractors. FAR 3.502(d)(1) allows the contracting officer to offset the amount of any kickback made to or by a subcontractor against amounts due the prime contractor under its government contract and direct the prime contractor to withhold the amount of any such kickback from payments due the subcontractor. FAR 3.502(g) requires the prime contractor and/or the subcontractor to report any suspected violation of this prohibition to the agency inspector general.

LOBBYING

FAR 52.203-12, entitled "Limitation on Payments to Influence Certain Federal Transactions," prohibits a federal contractor from using "appropriated funds" to pay any person attempting to influence or influencing any officer or employee of an agency, a member of Congress, an officer or employee of Congress in connection with any covered federal actions, such as awarding, extending, or modifying a contract. In other words, a contractor cannot use funds received in payment for performing under the contract for lobbying purposes if the original source of those payments received under the contract was funding appropriated by Congress to the contracting agency. The term "appropriated funds" does not include profit in the contract, so contractors are free to use their own profit to retain lobbyists if they so choose.

Using Suspended or Debarred Subcontractors

Another standard clause is FAR 52.209-6, "Protecting the Government's Interest when Subcontracting with Contractors Debarred, Suspended, or Proposed for Debarment." This clause mandates that, except for commercially available off-the-shelf items, a contractor not enter into any subcontract with a value exceeding $30,000 with any firm that is suspended, debarred, or proposed for debarment. Whenever a contractor is about to issue a subcontract exceeding $30,000 (except a subcontract for a commercially available off-the-shelf item), the contractor is required to have the proposed subcontractor certify that neither it nor its principals are suspended, debarred, or proposed for debarment.

Employment of Former Government Officials

In addition to the Procurement Integrity Act provisions discussed above, there are certain restrictions on employment of government officials after they leave their government jobs. While most of those restrictions apply to the employee, if a contract is with the Department of Defense (DOD), the clause DFAR 252.203-7000, "Requirements Relating to Compensation of Former DOD Officials," will be included. It prohibits a DOD contractor from "knowingly" providing compensation to certain covered DOD officials (generally executive level or senior executive level procurement officials) within two years of the official leaving government service, without first determining that the official has sought and received an opinion from the DOD ethics counselor concerning any post-employment restrictions. Failure on a contractor's part to comply with this clause can result in the government rescinding the contract as well as possible suspension or debarment.

PROHIBITION AGAINST EMPLOYMENT OF CERTAIN CONVICTED FELONS

Another clause offerors will find in DOD solicitations is 252.203-7001, "Prohibition on Persons Convicted of Fraud or Other Defense-Contractor Related Felonies." This clause prohibits any person convicted of fraud or any other felony arising out of a DOD contract from serving in a management or supervisory capacity on any DOD contract; on the contractor's board of directors; as a contractor consultant, agent, or representative; or in any other capacity that can "influence, advise, or control" decisions in connection with the contract.

Unless waived, this ban lasts for no less than five years from the date of the conviction. If a contractor knowingly employs someone in violation of this restriction or allows them to serve on the board of directors, or the board of directors of a "first-tier" subcontractor (a subcontractor whose subcontract is directly with the contractor), the contractor is subject to a criminal penalty of no more than $500,000, as well as suspension or debarment and cancellation of the contract at no cost to the government. Contractors are required to include the substance of this clause in all first-tier subcontracts that exceed the Simplified Acquisition Threshold, except subcontracts for commercial items or components.

REQUIREMENT FOR A CONTRACTOR CODE OF BUSINESS ETHICS AND CONDUCT

If the solicitation on which an offeror competing contemplates a contract that will exceed $5 million and require more than 120 days to perform, it will include the clause at FAR 52.203-13, "Contractor Code of Business Ethics and Conduct." This clause requires that within thirty days after contract award, the contractor must implement a code of business ethics and conduct, and provide it to all of its employees performing on the contract. The clause also includes a requirement that it be incorporated in any subcontract that also exceeds the $5 million/120 day threshold (meaning that subcontractor would also have to implement such a code of conduct).

DISPLAY OF HOTLINE POSTER

A solicitation may also include the clause at FAR 52.203-14 (mandatory for contracts that are not for commercial items and are expected to exceed $5 million). This clause requires the contractor to display "prominently" in its facility (and any off-site work locations) the procuring agency's official poster with the agency's hotline for reporting fraud in performance of the contract. The contracting officer will include in the solicitation the location from which the posters can be obtained.

WHISTLEBLOWER PROTECTIONS

Everyone has almost certainly read stories in the media about "whistleblowers" reporting on fraud by their government contractor employers. The federal government has issued regulations protecting contractor employees who report on such improper activity.

FAR 3.903 makes it federal policy that contractors not "discharge, demote, or otherwise discriminate" against an employee as a "reprisal for disclosing information to a Member of Congress, or [the Department of Justice]" involving a "substantial violation of law related to a [federal] contract (including the competition for or negotiation of a contract)." Any employee who believes he or she has been retaliated against may file a complaint with the agency's Inspector General, who is charged with inquiring into the complaint and, if deemed necessary, launching a full-fledged investigation. If the investigation sustains the complaint, the contractor can be forced to abate the reprisal, including reinstating the person to his or her prior position, paying back pay (plus benefits), and paying all of the complaining employee's expenses reasonably incurred in connection with the complaint.

Exclusion from Government Contracting

The concepts of suspension and debarment are unique to government contracting, including federal, state, and local. Basically they are formal procedures by which a government can exclude a contractor from receiving government contracts for a set period of time, generally up to three years (although contracts on which the contractor is performing generally are not affected). Each contracting agency has procedures governing suspension and debarment, designed to afford some degree of due process, since when contractors are suspended or debarred (or proposed for debarment), the names will be published for everyone to see on a government website listing companies and individuals who are excluded from federal contracting.

Suspension

The federal government has the right to suspend a contractor from government contracting if criminal or administrative proceedings are initiated against that contractor by the federal government or any state or local government. Generally, the types of criminal or administrative proceeding that will result in a suspension are those involving acts of dishonesty, as opposed to acts that are technically criminal (drunk driving, for example). When a contractor is suspended, it is immediately ineligible for the award of federal contracts (including those on which it has bids or offers pending) and its name is posted on the government website. The suspension will generally remain in effect until the criminal or administrative proceedings are resolved, assuming those proceedings are resolved in the contractor's favor. In the event they are not resolved in the contractor's favor, the suspension will be converted to a debarment (usually with "credit" for the "time served" during the suspension period).

Debarment

Debarment is the formal term used when the federal government opts to bar a contractor from contracting with it for a set period of time, generally a maximum of three (3) years. Debarment proceedings can be brought as a result of a criminal conviction or administrative ruling against a company, but they can also be initiated if the company has a persistent record of poor performance on its federal contracts. Agency debarment regulations provide that the contractor must receive a "Notice of Proposed Debarment" listing the reasons for the proposed action and the supporting evidence. The contractor will have the right to respond in writing and to appear before the debarring official to contest the action, if it chooses (although a contractor is not permitted to challenge the evidence if the debarment is based on a criminal conviction, since it will already have had its "day in court" in the form of the criminal trial). Be aware, though, that much like the case of a suspension, a contractor is ineligible for the award of government contracts the moment it receives the notice. While that may seem unfair, the government's position is that no one has the right to a government contract and debarment is not punishment, but is designed to protect the government.

REPORTING EXECUTIVE COMPENSATION AND FIRST-TIER SUBCONTRACT AWARDS

Unless and until a small business becomes a very successful contractor, the first part of this requirement, contained in the clause at FAR 52.204-10, Reporting Executive Compensation and First-Tier Subcontract Awards, will likely not be applicable. As part of their annual SAM registration, companies that in the prior year received 80 percent of their revenues from federal grants or contracts (including subcontracts), and if those revenues exceeded $25 million, are required to report the compensation (including all forms of compensation) of their five (5) highest paid executives. There is no limit or cap on what those executives can receive in compensation; the clause merely requires that the compensation be reported for public access on a government website. A company need not comply with this requirement, however, if the information is publicly available elsewhere (such as an SEC filing for a publicly traded company).

The part of the clause that will likely come into play, irrespective of the amount of revenues a contractor derives from the federal government, is the requirements in (d)(2) and perhaps (d)(3). Under (d)(2), by the end of the month after the award of a "first-tier" subcontract ("first-tier" referring to a contract that awarded directly by the government contractor to another company), the contractor is required to report all such subcontracts awarded that exceeded $25,000, including specific information relating to each. These reports are to be filed at www.fsrs.gov, and the website provides instructions. There are two exceptions to this reporting requirement. If in the contractor's previous tax year the contractor's gross revenues from all sources were less than $300,000, the contractor is not required to report subcontract awards. If the subcontractor had gross revenues in its previous tax year from all sources that were less than $300,000, that subcontract award need not be reported.

The second, and perhaps more difficult requirement, is the one at (d)(3) in the clause. For each first-tier subcontract that is reported on the government website, the contractor is required to report the compensation of the subcontractor's five highest paid executives if that subcontractor met the 80 percent/$25 million threshold and that information was not otherwise publicly available. In other words, it will be the prime contractor's responsibility to procure this information from any of its subcontractors who meet the threshold, even if the prime contractor itself does not. Of course, getting this information may prove easier said than done if the subcontractor is privately owned. It might be a good idea for a prime contractor to include this clause in any subcontracts awarded under the prime contract before requesting this information from a subcontractor.

CONCLUSION

The government takes its ethics requirements for contractors very seriously. Ignoring the ethical obligations mandated by contractual clauses and FAR provisions can have serious and long-term negative consequences. It is extremely rare to see a small business contractor survive the standard three-year debarment period, and potential fines and/or penalties can easily drive even a financially healthy small business into bankruptcy. As a government contractor, the onus is on you to know your ethical obligations and adhere to them strictly.

Chapter 4

SOCIOECONOMIC PROGRAMS

The Government has many specific programs targeted toward small businesses with the goal of increasing their share of federal contracting dollars. In fact, you may qualify for more than one such program. The Small Business Administration (SBA) is the agency created by Congress and tasked with carrying out programs designed to foster the growth of small businesses in the United States. Many programs, such as loan guarantees, do not involve government contracting (at least not directly) and so are outside the purview of this book. However, if you are a small business and hopeful of getting into government contracting, there are SBA programs that can definitely assist you.

SMALL BUSINESS SET-ASIDES

SBA is the agency that establishes the rules that determine what constitutes a small business. The "size standards" are pegged to the North American Industry Classification System (NAICS) codes. If a business has a manufacturing NAICS code, its size status will be determined by the number of people it employs, averaged over a fifty-two-week period back from the date of the determination. For some NAICS codes, a business with a thousand employees is still considered small, while for others, it is much less. If a business is in a service industry, its size status will be determined by its average revenues for the preceding three years. Depending on the particular NAICS code, a business might be limited to $7 million in average revenues to be considered small, whereas for other codes, $27 million or $33 million in revenue might still qualify as "small." Size standards are reviewed annually and adjusted up or down by the SBA in order to maintain an adequate number of qualifying small businesses.

Under federal law, there is what is generally called the "Rule of Two." What this means is that a contracting officer intending to initiate competition for a particular product or service expected to exceed the Simplified Acquisition Threshold must first conduct market research to determine if there is a reasonable expectation that at least two (2) responsible small businesses are likely to submit bids to supply the goods or services and that the award can be expected to be made at a reasonable price. Market research is generally accomplished by posting a "Sources Sought" notice on the

FedBizOps website, which is another powerful reason for small businesses to monitor that website. If responses to a "Sources Sought" notice demonstrate that there are likely to be two such responsible small businesses and the award can be expected to be made at a reasonable price, than the procurement must be issued as a "Small Business Set-Aside," which, as the name suggests, means that only small businesses are eligible to compete.

Even where the quantity of a given item to be purchased is significantly large, so that it makes it unlikely that any small business could offer on the requirement, let alone perform, that is no justification for refusing to conduct a small business set-aside competition. If the quantity of an item being procured can be broken down into two or more parts, one part is to be procured as "unrestricted," while the other is to be restricted to small businesses. This is known as a partial set-aside. The decision on whether to set a particular procurement aside exclusively for small business competitors is generally left to the discretion of the contracting officer, and that discretion will not be disturbed unless it has been found to have been abused. One area more likely to be reviewed is a decision not to conduct a partial set-aside. As with anything else, there are exceptions, but the purpose of the "Rule of Two" is to favor small businesses in government contracting.

The procedure for conducting small business set-aside procurements begins with the contracting officer. It is the contracting officer, in the first instance, who selects the NAICS code most appropriate for the particular procurement. Given the disparity in size standards among NAICS codes, the choice of a code for a competition can have a significant effect. Under one NAICS code, a firm may qualify as a small business eligible to compete, while under another it may be considered large and therefore ineligible. It is for that reason that SBA regulations allow for potential offerors to appeal the contracting officer's choice of NAICS code to SBA's Office of Hearings and Appeals, which will then have the final say on the matter.

Offering on a Small Business Set-Aside Procurement

When submitting an offer in a small business set-aside competition, the offeror will be required to certify that it is, in fact, small. That certification, accomplished by checking the appropriate block in the solicitation form, will normally be accepted unless the contracting officer has reason to believe otherwise, or unless another offeror challenges the firm's status by way of what is called a size protest (see Chapter 9, Contract Awards and Competition Controversies). Such challenges are decided by way of the SBA then doing what is called a "size determination." Offerors need to be very aware that a false certification can have major consequences. Any certification in an offer that is false (and there are numerous certifications in addition to size status) violates a federal criminal statute, 18 U.S.C. § 1001. It can result in criminal prosecution of an individual or company and possible debarment from Federal contracting. Also, if an offeror wins a small business set-aside contract and is later found to have falsely certified its status, SBA regulations establish a legal presumption that the government's damages arising from the false certification are equal to the full amount of the contract. In other words, the government is permitted to retain the products delivered or the benefit of the services provided, and still come after the contractor to recover the money it was paid.

Under SBA's regulations, when a contractor receives a small business set-aside contract, its size is set at the time of the award. In other words, for purposes of that contract, the contractor is considered small for the duration, regardless of its actual size. Thus, the government can exercise options even when a contractor is no longer small. What about multi-award situations, where the contract calls for subsequent competitions for task or work orders? Unless the solicitation for that particular task or work order competition calls for an offeror to recertify its small business status, the offeror will still be considered small for that competition based on the original award.

When an agency proposes to award a contract arising out of a small business set-aside competition, it is required to provide a three-day advance notice to all bidders or offerors. This is to allow the other competitors an opportunity to challenge the small business status of the would-be awardee. This is not the same as the notice that is to be provided after an award is made. This notice is designed specifically for protests regarding size status (again, see Chapter 9). It is important to remember that in the case of a small business set-aside competition, an offeror must still be small at the time of the contract award in order to be eligible to receive the contract.

Subcontracting Under Small Business Set-Aside Contracts

Contractors need to be aware of a couple of other points when they go after small business set-aside contract awards. There are clauses that restrict the small business contractor's right to subcontract the work. The government does not want small businesses acting as "fronts" for large businesses by winning contracts and then turning around and subcontracting the work to a large business. For example, the "Limitations on Subcontracting" (FAR 52.219.14) defines the percentage of the work that the contractor must perform itself. The "Limitations in Subcontracting" clause does not apply if the contractor considered a dealer in the item being procured. The FAR clause "Notice of Small Business Set-Aside" (2.219-6), included in all small business set-aside solicitations, allows a firm to bid on small business set-asides as a dealer under what is known as the "non-manufacturer rule," subject to the "Agreement" included in the clause that the contractor agree, in advance, to supply only products produced by small businesses in the United States. Subcontracting part of the work to a large business is allowed, but the end product must be considered to be the product of a small business. In other words, a bidder competing as a "dealer" in a particular product does not have to do any of the labor; however, the products it delivers to the government must still be produced by small businesses in the U.S.

The Certificate of Competency Program

A small business competing for government contracts may, at some point, need to avail itself of SBA's Certificate of Competency (COC) Program. Under this program, any small business that is denied a contract award for "responsibility" issues, such as finances, for example, or plant capacity, has the right to have that denial reviewed by way of an application to the SBA for a COC. SBA will do a complete review of the company (including a size determination) and the bid or offer and then render a decision. If SBA issues the COC, the contracting officer must award that firm the contract at issue.

The 8(a) Program

This is an SBA Program designed to assist minority-owned small businesses that were historically unable to win government contracts due to social or economic discrimination, in gaining access to government contract awards. Under the program, formally known as the 8(a) Business Development Program, minority-owned small businesses are assisted by having some procurements set aside exclusively for competition among program participants. Additionally directed contract awards (awards made without competition) are authorized. These are usually awarded to firms that market themselves and their capabilities to contracting agencies and to SBA. In the case of a directed award, the contract is actually awarded to SBA, which then issues a subcontract to the selected firm. Unlike a normal subcontracting arrangement, though, once the subcontract is awarded, for all practical purposes SBA drops out of the picture.

Unlike small business status, a business seeking to avail itself of the benefits of the 8(a) Program cannot simply certify itself as qualified; it must be certified by SBA for admission. To qualify, the company must be small and unconditionally (majority) owned and controlled by one or more socially and economically disadvantaged U.S. citizens. Persons in certain ethnic groups are presumed to be socially disadvantaged based on a past history of discrimination, including African Americans, Hispanics, American Indians, Alaskan Indians, and Asian Pacific Americans. Individuals not in any of these ethnic groups may also qualify as socially disadvantaged, but are required to demonstrate to SBA that they, as individuals, have been discriminated against. Such individual discrimination may be based on gender or a physical handicap, as examples. To qualify as economically disadvantaged at the time of an initial application for admission to the 8(a) Program, the qualifying individual must have a net worth no greater than $250,000 (not counting equity in his or her home and equity in the business). For continued participation, the qualifying individual's net worth (not counting equity in his or her home and equity in the business) may not exceed $750,000. SBA also requires the applicant to prove that the business has the "potential for success" by requiring it to have been in business for at least two years prior to applying, although the two-year requirement can be waived if the applicant can demonstrate its potential for success.

Additionally, SBA will look long and hard at whether the applicant is, in fact, owned and controlled by the qualifying minority owner. Control must be both day-to-day and overall. Merely showing that the qualifying minority owns a 51 percent interest in the business is not enough. Over the years the 8(a) Program was replete with fraud in the form of participating firms that had minority owners who were "front men" while the firms were in fact controlled by non-minority businessmen. One common tactic was to have a qualifying minority who owned 51 percent of the business, but the firm's bylaws required a 60 percent "super majority" for any major decisions, such as setting salaries or borrowing money. Any limitation on the right of the 51 percent owner to control the business will sink the application.

Participation in the 8(a) Program is not perpetual (although special rules apply to firms owned by American Indian or Alaskan Indian tribes). Firms are limited to nine (9) years of participation. During the first four (4) years, participants are considered to be in the "developmental" stage of their participation; years five through nine are the "transition" stage. During the developmental stage, participants are eligible to participate as a protégé in SBA's Mentor-Protégé Program. Under the Mentor-Protégé Program, a participant and its mentor can bid as a Joint Venture (see Chapter 5, Teaming Agreements) on any government contract, even if the Mentor is a large business.

So what happens when a small business that is not a Program participant wants to pursue a contract that is suddenly placed in the 8(a) Program? There are certain restrictions on SBA accepting a requirement for a directed 8(a) award or a competition limited to certified 8(a) firms. SBA cannot accept a requirement for the 8(a) Program when doing so would have an adverse impact on a small business or group of small businesses. Unless the requirement is considered "new," prior to accepting the opportunity for the 8(a) Program, SBA must do an "adverse impact analysis." Adverse impact is presumed where (1) a small business has been performing the requirement at the time it is offered to SBA for at least twenty-four months, (2) is performing it at the time of the offer to SBA (or completed performance within thirty days of the offer), and (3) the requirement accounts for 25 percent or more of that firm's most recent annual gross sales.

HUBZone Contracting

HUBZone stands for Historically Underutilized Business Zone. It refers to areas that traditionally have suffered from high unemployment. HUBZones are determined by the Census Bureau after each regular census. If a business is located in a census tract that is designated a HUBZone, it is eligible to apply for HUBZone certification (like the 8(a) Program, SBA must approve your admission to the program). To qualify for the HUBZone Program, in addition to being located in a HUBZone (and bear in mind that HUBZones are re-determined after every census; a firm may be in a HUBZone and then a few years later no longer in a HUBZone), a business must meet the following requirements: it must be small under its NAICS code, it must be majority-owned and controlled by "persons" who are U.S. citizens (in this instance "persons" actually means living persons, as opposed to a corporation or other type of business entity), and 35 percent of its employees must live in a HUBZone (although not necessarily the same HUBZone as the business). For purposes of the HUBZone determination, an "employee" is a person who works a minimum of forty hours per month. The term includes employees obtained from a temporary employee agency, leasing concern, or through a union agreement or co-employed pursuant to a professional employer organization agreement.

There is no time limit on HUBZone status. So long as a firm's location remains in a census tract designated a HUBZone and it continues to meet the other requirements (i.e., remaining a small business 51 percent owned by U.S. citizens and the 35 percent employee residency requirements), the firm may continue as a certified HUBZone contractor. HUBZone contractors are required, however, to "re-certify" to SBA within thirty days after the third anniversary of their original certification, and then every three years thereafter that they continue to be in compliance with all HUBZone Program requirements.

The first type of contracting aid to HUBZone contractors is by way of set-aside competitions. Contracting agencies are authorized to designate certain procurements as set aside exclusively for competition among bidders who are participants in the HUBZone Program. The second type of aid to HUBZone businesses is a 10 percent evaluation preference. A federal statute mandates that in any unrestricted procurement, a 10 percent "evaluation preference" be applied to offers from HUBZone bidders. In such a competition, if a HUBZone bidder is within 10 percent of the price of the low bidder and that low bidder is a large business, 10 percent is added to the large business's price for purposes of determining who the low bidder is.

Remember, though, this only applies when the low bidder is a large business; the evaluation preference does not apply if the low bidder is another small business. In other words, a HUBZone small business does not get an advantage over another small business.

Service-Disabled Veteran-Owned/ Veteran-Owned Contracting

This program provides contracting assistance to small businesses owned and controlled by service-disabled veterans and veterans. With the exception of the Department of Veterans Affairs (VA), contracting agencies are permitted (but not required) to conduct procurements limited to Service-Disabled Veteran-Owned Small Businesses (SDVOSBs) or Veteran-Owned Small Businesses (VOSBs). For the VA, on the other hand, SDVOSB and VOSB contracting is mandatory. Before a solicitation can be issued, the VA contracting officer must determine if there are two (2) or more SDVOSBs who can be expected to bid. If so, the procurement must be restricted to SDVOSBs. If there are not two (2) SDVOSBs, VOSBs must be considered next. Only if there are not two (2) VOSBs expected to bid can the solicitation be released as open to non-SDVOSB/VOSB bidders. To qualify for SDVOSB/VOSB contracting, the firm must be small and must be majority-owned and controlled by one or more service-disabled veterans (in the case of a VOSB, veterans). There is no "economically disadvantaged" requirement.

Another important distinction between SDVOSB and VOSB contracting at the VA and at other agencies is that, in the case of other agencies, bidders are allowed to self-certify that they are a qualified SDVOSB or VOSB. The VA, on the other hand, requires SDVOSBs and VOSBs to be certified by its Center for Veteran Enterprise (CVE). Similar to the situation that plagued the 8(a) Program in its early days, the VA program for SDVOSB and VOSB set-asides was replete with firms "fronted" by veterans who had little or nothing to do with running the business. In some cases, veterans "marketed" their status to firms in exchange for a certain percentage of the contract revenue. Today, to participate in the VA set-aside program, a firm must be certified by the CVE, and the CVE does not simply accept that a veteran "controls" the business because he or she owns 51 percent. The CVE will, of course look to verify that the veteran's majority ownership is not limited somehow, but the CVE will also look to determine that the majority-owner veteran has the educational background, training, or experience necessary to run the business. If the CVE concludes that the veteran lacks that education, training, or experience, it will deny certification for lack of "control" over the business. Also, status as a SDVOSB or VOSB can be challenged by another bidder (see Chapter 9, Contract Awards and Competition Controversies).

Economically Disadvantaged Woman-Owned Small Business and Woman-Owned Small Business Contracting.

A recently created program provides for agencies to conduct procurements restricted to Economically Disadvantaged Woman-Owned Small Businesses (EDWOSBs) and Woman-Owned Small Businesses (WOSBs). The SDWOSB and WOSB

Program is administered by SBA and, like the 8(a) Program, requires firms to apply for admission. Requirements are similar to the 8(a) Program, although to qualify as economically disadvantaged, the business owner must have a net worth of less than $750,000, excluding her personal residence and her equity in the business, rather than the $250,000 required at the time of the initial application for admission to the 8(a) Program. SBA will also consider the personal income of the applicant; if her adjusted gross income for the three years preceding the application exceeded $350,000, SBA will presume she is not economically disadvantaged. SBA may also consider the applicant's spouse's financial situation and may require financial information from the spouse unless the two are legally separated. Finally, similar to the requirements established for the 8(a) Program, the qualifying woman owner must control the day-to-day and long-term business operations.

CONTRACTUAL REQUIREMENTS

In addition to formal government programs designed to assist small businesses, contractors will find that many government solicitations have clauses that require, in the event a firm receives the contract, the establishment of various internal programs to be followed in the hiring of employees. Among these are FAR 52.222-21 (Prohibition of Segregated Facilities), 52.222-23 (Notice of Requirement for Affirmative Action to Ensure Equal Employment Opportunity for Construction), 52.222-25 (Affirmative Action Compliance), 52.222-26 (Equal Opportunity), 52.222-35 (Equal Opportunity for Veterans), 52.222-36 (Affirmative Action for Workers with Disabilities) and 52.222-54 (Employment Eligibility Verification). All of these clauses are designed to carry out policies in laws enacted by Congress or executive orders issued by the president, and in most cases the clauses require contractors to submit reports or maintain records showing compliance.

Another contract-related small business program is the requirement in unrestricted procurements (ones where any size business can submit a bid), which all large business bidders include as part of their bids a "Small Business Subcontracting Plan." The plan sets out what percentage of the contract work will be subcontracted to small businesses, minority-owned small businesses, woman-owned small businesses, etc. In many cases, a solicitation will state a specific percentage of the work that large businesses are to subcontract to small businesses. The contracting officer is required to monitor the large business contractor's achievement of its goals.

THE SMALL BUSINESS INNOVATION RESEARCH PROGRAM

The Small Business Innovation Research (SBIR) Program is a competitive program created by the Small Business Innovation Development Act of 1982, and designed to encourage small businesses to engage in research and development (R&D) that has the potential for commercialization. Through the process of competitive awards, small businesses have the opportunity to participate in R&D efforts and to profit from the commercialization of the results of those efforts. The SBIR Program goals are: (1) stimulate technological innovation; (2) use small businesses to meet federal R&D needs; (3) encourage participation in innovation by socially and economically disadvantaged firms; and (4) increase commercialization of innovations developed through federal R&D efforts. Federal agencies with outside R&D budgets exceeding $100 million are required to allocate a certain percentage of their budget to the SBIR Program. Among the regularly participating agencies are the Department of Defense (DOD), the Department of Energy (DOE), the Department of Homeland Security (DHS), the Department of Health and Human Services (DHHS), the National Aeronautics and Space Administration (NASA), the Environmental Protection Agency (EPA), and the National Science Foundation (NSF). Each agency has an SBIR Program office that administers the program in accordance with guidelines established by Congress in the Small Business Act and by SBA in its SBIR Policy Directive (SBA does not actually administer the program, though). A participating agency will designate R&D topics in solicitations and accept proposals from small businesses in response. Awards are then made competitively.

A special benefit of the SBIR Program is that unlike a standard government contract where the government acquires unlimited rights to any technical data and computer software produced (see Chapter 11, Contract Performance Issues), the SBIR contractor maintains data rights to the technical data and computer software produced with contract funds for a minimum of four (4) years. These rights are set forth in the special FAR and DFAR clauses included in SBIR contracts: "Rights in Data-SBIR Program" (FAR 52.227-20) and "Rights in Noncommercial Data and Computer Software-Small Business Innovation Research (SBIR) Program" (DFAR 252.227-7018).

There are three phases to a SBIR contract. In Phase One, the scientific and technical merit, feasibility, and commercial potential of the proposed R&D efforts is established, and the quality of the small business awardee's performance is determined prior to additional funding being provided. Phase One awards are generally limited to $150,000 and six months' duration. Phase Two is for the continuation of the R&D efforts begun in Phase One. Additional funding is based on the results achieved in Phase One regarding scientific and technical merit and commercial potential. Phase Two awards are generally limited to $1,000,000 and a two-year performance period. In Phase Three the small business awardee is to pursue commercialization objectives developed in Phases One and Two. The SBIR Program does not fund Phase Three efforts, although some agencies may provide non-SBIR funding for production contracts for products or services intended for use by the U.S. Government. A Phase Three contract may be awarded to a Phase One or Phase Two contractor even if it is no longer a small business.

The Small Business Technology Transfer Program

The Small Business Technology Transfer Program (STTR) differs from the SBIR Program. It is designed to expand funding in the innovation area by creating joint venture opportunities between small businesses and nonprofit research institutions. The goals of the STTR Program are the same as those for the SBIR Program: (1) stimulate technological innovation; (2) use small businesses to meet federal R&D needs; (3) encourage participation in innovation by socially and economically disadvantaged firms; and (4) increase commercialization of innovations developed through federal R&D efforts. Under the STTR Program, the small business is to collaborate with a research institution in Phases One and Two. Unlike the SBIR Program, there are strict requirements regarding allocation of the work. The small business must perform at least 40 percent of the work, while the research institution must perform at least 30 percent. In addition, participation in the STTR Program requires that the small business and the research institution enter into an intellectual property agreement, detailing allocation of intellectual property rights between the two parties, as well as the rights to carry out follow-up research, development, and commercialization efforts. Federal agencies with outside research budgets in excess of $1 billion participate in the STTR Program and are required to allocate a certain percentage of those dollars to it. Currently, participating agencies include DOD, DOE, DHHS, NASA, and NSF. As with the SBIR Program, an agency will designate R&D topics in a solicitation, accept proposals from small businesses in response thereto, and make awards competitively.

CONCLUSION

Government programs designed to aid small businesses, such as SBA's 8(a) and HUBZone Programs and the programs for certified veteran-owned and woman-owned set-aside competitions, can provide you with significant opportunities in pursuing federal contracts by allowing you to compete against other businesses of similar size and financial condition to your own. You should remember, too, that these programs are not mutually exclusive; you can participate in as many as you qualify for.

Chapter 5

TEAMING AGREEMENTS

The most common situation in bidding on government contracts is that of a single bidder submitting its bid or offer in response to an Invitation for Bids (IFB) or Request for Proposals (RFP). However, there are occasions where it can be beneficial or even necessary for two or more firms to create a team for purposes of competing. Such situations arise where contract performance would require a number of different disciplines. Common examples are contracts to manage Federal office buildings, which may require janitorial services, elevator maintenance, minor or major construction work, and full-time trades such as carpenters and electricians, or contracts that call for the manufacture of various items together with warehousing. Offering as a team may allow two small firms to "combine" their resources and abilities, enabling them to compete for a contract too large for either to have a chance of winning alone. Also, in many cases the experience and past performance of the different team members can be attributed to the team so as to enhance the team's ability to win the contract. In such situations, a number of companies may enter into a "teaming agreement," by which they agree to submit an offer on the contract as a team and specify the responsibilities of each team member during the proposal phase so that, in the event of an award, the roles and responsibilities of each team member have already been laid out. There are three common types of teaming arrangements used by government contractors: prime contractor/subcontractor, joint venture, and limited liability company. Each of these will be discussed in turn.

PRIME CONTRACTOR/SUBCONTRACTOR RELATIONSHIP

This type of teaming arrangement is the most common one. One member of the team submits the bid or proposal in its name alone. In the event of a contract award, the contract will be solely in the name of that team member, who will be considered by the government to be the contractor. For purposes of the team, that firm is referred to as the "prime contractor." The remaining team members would all be subcontractors. In this type of arrangement, each member's profits and losses are their own. The prime contractor may make money while the subcontractors lose money and vice versa.

It is necessary to bear in mind that there are important implications in a prime contractor/subcontractor type of arrangement. For example, the prime contractor is the exclusive party for dealings with the government. Indeed, the contracting officer will in all likelihood refuse to even speak with a subcontractor without authorization from the prime contractor. The concept is called "privity of contract," meaning a direct contractual relation. This concept is strictly construed by the government, and contracting officers are instructed to deal only with an entity that is in "privity of contract" with the government. Also, the prime contractor bears sole responsibility for contract performance. In the event of a failure of performance by a subcontractor, the government will look to the prime contractor to remedy that failure and hold the prime contractor solely responsible in the event the failure is not remedied. If non-performance by a subcontractor results in a termination for default being issued by the government (see Chapter 10, Contract Administration), it will be the prime contractor that suffers the default termination on its record and it is the prime contractor who will be responsible for any re-procurement damages assessed by the government. Failure on the part of a subcontractor does not provide the prime contractor with an excuse or a defense to a default termination.

From the subcontractors' perspective, the corresponding situation is that a subcontractor has no rights versus the government, as the subcontractor and the government are not in "privity of contract." In the event the prime contractor fails to pay the subcontractor and there is no payment bond in place (as is generally required for construction contracts), unless the government has agreed specifically to protect the subcontractor's position, the subcontractor cannot seek payment directly from the government. Additionally, a subcontractor cannot avail itself of the disputes process set out in the prime contract (see Chapter 13, Disputes) to pursue a claim against the government; again, lack of privity. Only a "contractor," meaning a party with an actual contract to which the government is a party, may pursue the contract's disputes process. A subcontractor seeking to press a claim against the government can only do so with the consent of and in the name of the prime contractor.

This lack of privity of contract does occasionally produce some absurd situations. For example, say a prime contractor subcontracts part of the performance of the contract work to another firm, which defaults on its obligations. The government then terminates the contract for default. In a commercial situation, the defaulted prime contractor could sue the government and join the defaulting subcontractor in the suit, seeking indemnification in the event the default termination is upheld by the court. In the world of government contracts, though, the defaulted prime contractor cannot get the government and the subcontractor in a single courtroom. The suit against the government can only be heard by the Court of Federal Claims or an agency board of contract appeals. Neither forum allows for the prime contractor to compel the joinder of a subcontractor as an additional defendant. If the suit against the government fails and the default termination is upheld, the prime contractor will then, of course, file suit against the defaulting subcontractor in a local court. However, the ruling in the first suit that the default termination was proper is not binding on the second court, since the subcontractor was not a party in the first suit. The subcontractor could argue that the default termination was not proper and could potentially prevail.

An advantage to using the prime contractor/subcontractor teaming arrangement is that, unlike the joint venture and limited liability formats discussed below, so long as the arrangement is a legitimate one (meaning the small business prime contractor is not merely acting as a front for a large business to win a small business set-aside contract), the team members are not lumped together for small business size purposes. In a prime contractor/subcontractor arrangement, the prime contractor, if it is a small business, can have large business subcontractors without losing its own small business status for the particular procurement. The only rule is that for small business set-aside manufacturing contracts, all the end-items delivered to the government must be products of one or more small businesses. While the prime contractor can have large business subcontractors on its team, the large businesses cannot produce the actual end-items being delivered to the government. Care must also be taken to structure the team so that, even aside from production of the end-items, the team is not "unduly reliant" on a large business subcontractor to perform the contract. The Small Business Administration (SBA) refers to that as the "Ostensible Subcontractor Rule," and a finding by SBA that the offeror was "unduly reliant" on the large business subcontractor would result in the offeror being declared ineligible for the particular small business set-aside procurement.

Conducting the Negotiations and Performing on the Contract

Once an offer is submitted in a prime contractor/subcontractor type of arrangement, the company that is designated the prime contractor in the teaming agreement is responsible for dealing with the government during the competition, in discussions, for example. Technically, the team member who submitted the bid or offer in its name is not required to consult with the other team members in dealing with the government during the competitive process unless the teaming agreement requires it. Regardless of the relative positions in the prospective team, i.e., prime contractor or a subcontractor, it makes sense for the agreement to spell out what input, if any, the proposed subcontractors will have in the event the government decides to conduct negotiations. It will help avoid disputes later.

Once the team member who submitted the bid or proposal receives the award as prime contractor, there will need to be subcontract agreements signed by all the members of the team. Contractors should bear in mind, though, that most contracts give the government the right to approve of the subcontractors. The fact that a proposed subcontractor is part of the team will ease the process of approval, but the government still must approve the use of each subcontractor. It is for that reason that when I prepare subcontract agreements for clients, I make the agreement conditional on the government's approval of that subcontractor for performance under the contract.

It is wise to have the terms of the agreements hammered out prior to submission of the offer. The team members should agree on the subcontract terms up front, if possible, and then incorporate the form into the teaming agreement by way of an exhibit. The team members do not want to be arguing over the terms of subcontract agreements when there has just been a contract award and performance is scheduled to commence. From the other perspective, a proposed subcontractor would also want the subcontract established in advance. Without something in the teaming agreement nailing down its position as a subcontractor in the event of an award to the prime contractor, nothing stops that prime contracting from looking for someone to do the work at a lower price.

Terms for a Subcontract Agreement

The terms of a subcontract agreement merit mention and careful consideration on the team's part. As we have discussed, government solicitations include dozens (if not hundreds) of clauses spelled out in full or incorporated by reference. Some of those clauses must be included in subcontracts (referred to as "flow down"), such as The Contractor Code of Business Ethics and Conduct (FAR 52.203-13), which must be included in any subcontract that has a value of over $500,000 and requires more than 120 days for performance, or Anti-Kickback Procedures (FAR 52.203-7), which must be included in any subcontract exceeding $150,000 in value. The team will want to consult with an attorney experienced in government contracting to ensure that all the mandatory clauses have been included in the subcontracts.

Over and above those clauses that must be included, there are several that a prime contractor would be wise to include. A good example is the Termination for Convenience of the Government clause (FAR 52.249-2). That clause, as I will discuss in depth in Chapter 10, allows the government to terminate a contract at any time, without being found to have breached it. Under the clause, the prime contractor can only recover the costs incurred in performing on the terminated portion, plus profit on those costs; unearned profits can never be recovered. If the government terminates the prime contract for convenience, forcing the prime contractor to terminate its subcontractors, and the termination for convenience clause was made part of their subcontracts, the same rules for recouping costs applies to the subcontractors. The government will reimburse the prime contractor for its costs in settling with its subcontractors in accordance with the same rules for recovery. If the prime contractor failed to make the termination for convenience clause part of the subcontracts, the subcontractors can sue the prime contractor for breach of contract as a result of the government's termination action. The subcontractors could conceivably recover their lost profits from the prime contractor, even though the prime contractor's recovery from the government would still be limited to what is allowed under the termination for convenience clause.

Likewise, the Government Delay of Work clause (FAR 52.242-17) and Changes clause (FAR 52.243-1) are ones a prime contractor will want to include in any subcontract. The former clause limits the government's liability for damages in the event of a government-caused delay to recovery of lost overhead, while the latter allows the government to make changes in work under the contract with the revised contract price to be determined through the process known as "Equitable Adjustment." If a prime contractor has not made these clauses part of its subcontracts, its exposure to its subcontractors in the event the government delays performance or makes changes in the work could be virtually unlimited.

Once again, a prime contractor will want to consult with an attorney experienced in government contracts to determine what clauses should be incorporated into its subcontracts. I might note that some years ago I prepared a standard form of subcontract agreement for use by my clients. The standard form lays out the responsibilities of the parties and the basic terms of their obligations to each other. There is then a schedule attached listing the various clauses from the particular prime contract that are then incorporated by reference into the subcontract (with the appropriate changes, such as substituting "prime contractor" where the FAR clause says "government," and subcontractor" where the clause says "contractor").

Joint Venture Relationship

Another common type of teaming arrangement for pursing government contracts is a joint venture. A joint venture is, in its purest form, a partnership between two or more firms created to perform work on a specific project (although the "partners" are usually referred to as "venturers" or "co-venturers"). A proposal submitted by a joint venture would be submitted in a name such as "ABC, Inc. and XYZ Corp., a Joint Venture." When the project is completed (or in the event the joint venture does not receive the award), the joint venture dissolves. In a joint venture, one venturer assumes the role of "Managing Venturer," with the primary responsibility for interacting with the government and overseeing performance of any contract awarded to the joint venture. The contract, though, is awarded to the joint venture, separate and apart from the venturers themselves. An employee of the Managing Venturer is usually designated "Project Manager," and that person is the one who will serve as conduit for communications between the joint venture and the government. While one venturer may be designated Managing Venturer, all the venturers share responsibility for contract performance, the same as if the contract had been awarded to a partnership. Because all the venturers share responsibility for contract performance, in the event Managing Venturer (or any venturer for that matter) files for bankruptcy protection and ceases operating or otherwise drops out of the project, the remaining venturers will be expected to complete the contract. Even in the absence of the Managing Venturer, the remaining venturers must continue work, and they would be expected to provide any additional capital required to complete the work.

Also, unlike a prime contractor/subcontractor arrangement where each team member's profits and losses are its own, in a joint venture the venturers agree to share profits and losses just as they would in a partnership. Such profit and loss sharing may be allocated equally among the venturers, or they may choose to allocate profits and losses based on specified ownership interests in the joint venture.

Another factor to be kept in mind is the ramifications of the joint venture format on size. When companies offer as a joint venture, they are considered affiliated for that particular procurement. The venturers' employees or revenues, as applicable under the SBA Size Standards, are counted together for purposes of determining whether the joint venture qualifies as a small business to offer in a small business set-aside competition. Thus, it may be that in a case where two small businesses elect to offer as a joint venture on a small business set-aside procurement, even though each may be considered small under the size standards, the joint venture could be considered "large" and hence ineligible for that particular procurement. Also, unlike the prime contractor/subcontractor arrangement in certain limited cases (such as certain 8(a) Program Mentor-Protégé arrangements approved by the SBA), if one participant in the joint venture is a large business, then the joint venture is automatically considered a large business. However, since the joint venture would dissolve in the event it was excluded from award of the particular contract, the determination of "large" would not carry over to bids or offers the individual venturers may have submitted in other procurements. I should note, though, that SBA regulations limit joint ventures between the same companies to three in a two-year span. Beyond that, the companies will likely be considered affiliated for size purposes. This is another area where consulting with an attorney experienced in government contracting prior to creating a joint venture to compete for a procurement would be a wise idea.

Creating a Limited Liability Company

In some circumstances, joint venturers prefer to use a type of vehicle known as a limited liability company (LLC). An LLC is a form of partnership in which the partners do not have individual liability for the company's acts or debts, similar to the corporate business form. However, unlike a corporation, profits are generally taxed the same way as in the case of a standard partnership, meaning no double taxation. It is the LLC that submits the offer ("ABC, LLC"), and since it is considered an entity separate from its owners (called "members" in the case of a LLC), it is the LLC that receives the award and assumes the position of contractor. The LLC is solely responsible for contract performance. One advantage of the LLC arrangement, aside from protecting the members from liability for its debts, is that an LLC has perpetual existence. Unlike a true joint venture, the LLC does not cease to exist upon completion of a particular contract or project (or in the event it fails to receive the award). An LLC can continue to offer on multiple solicitations over an unlimited time period. It will remain in existence until dissolved by the members.

You should keep in mind that there are small business "size" implications in the use of the LLC arrangement, somewhat different from those in the case of a joint venture. The LLC is a company in its own right, having an existence separate from its owners. Thus its size would, in the first instance, be determined by the number of its own employees or the amount of its revenues, as appropriate. However, owners of an LLC are usually considered to control it for small business size purposes. When an LLC is controlled by one or more other companies or persons, the entire group could be considered affiliated for determining the LLC's size. In this scenario, unlike that of a joint venture (whose existence is limited to a single procurement or contract), were the LLC found by the Small Business Administration to be large, the determination could impact on the managing owners ("affiliates") and not be limited to the particular competition. Potential team members should be very careful in creating a LLC to ensure that the LLC and its managing owners, viewed as a group, do not result in the LLC being anything other than "small." One way to accomplish this is by having one member of the LLC own a majority interest and be designated as the "Managing Member." In this scenario, only the Managing Member would control the LLC, and so long as the Managing Member itself remains small, and the total employees or revenues of the managing member and the LLC do not exceed the size standard, the LLC should also remain small.

This is another area where consulting with an attorney experienced in government contracting is a must. A few years ago we were retained by a small business LLC that had been denied Service-Disabled Veteran-Owned Small Business certification (SDVOSB; see Chapter 4, Socioeconomic Programs). The principals had gotten a sample LLC operating agreement from the internet and simply filled in the blanks. Unfortunately, the regulations governing certification as a SDVOSB require that the LLC be "majority owned and controlled" by the qualifying disabled veteran, and the sample form the principals used called for all the members to have equal say in running the company. Naturally, the firm was denied certification. In order to fix the problem, we re-wrote the LLC operating agreement to make the majority ownership and control of the qualifying veteran crystal clear and unfettered. The firm eventually received its certification, but the time and effort expended in the original application had been totally wasted.

Conclusion

Teaming with other potential contractors, whether by way of a joint venture or prime contractor/subcontractor relationship, can greatly increase your chances of success in competitions for contracts such as managing or renovating federal facilities, or by allowing small business contractors in different trades to pool their experience, so as to demonstrate a past performance record that none of them could demonstrate on their own. Remember: a piece of a pie is better than no pie at all.

Chapter 6

COMPETITION METHODS

T he government employs many different methods for conducting competitions, in many cases depending on the types of products or services being procured. Each different method has its own section of the FAR with its own rules and guidelines. I will cover the major methods here.

ACQUISITION OF COMMERCIAL ITEMS (FAR PART 12)

FAR Part 12 instructs contracting agencies to conduct market research to determine whether a commercially available item or service will satisfy the government's needs. This harkens back to the efforts in the 1990s to have the government stop using the detailed specifications that resulted in $600 hammers and $400 toilet seats, in favor of the types of specifications used in the commercial world. A "commercial item" is defined in the FAR as an item (or service) which is of a type customarily used by the general public or non-governmental entities and that has been sold, leased, or licensed, or offered for sale, lease, or license to the general public. The FAR definition also states that minor modifications to an item sold or offered for sale to the public, made to accommodate the government's needs, do not alter the commercial nature of the item.

The latter part of the definition of "commercial item" ("sold" or "offered") creates an interesting conflict. Our office was contacted by a firm that had sold aircraft test stands to the U.S. military. It seems a contract had been lost to a competitor who had never actually produced a test stand, but who had posted design drawings for test stands on its website, inviting potential customers to inquire about purchasing one. We protested, questioning how someone who had never actually produced the item could "offer" it for sale. In the end we lost. The GAO and the Court of Federal Claims ruled that it was sufficient for someone to put up a website stating that the item was now being "offered" for sale, even without ever having produced a single one.

While there are exceptions for certain situations, contracts for commercial items are to be firm, fixed-price or firm, fixed-price with economic price adjustment (EPA). The standard government form for contracts (SF1449) is used, but the usual provisions are modified to conform to customary commercial practices. Additionally, contracting officers are authorized to consider government financing in connection with acquisition of commercial items (e.g., advance or interim payments), subject to proper security from the contractor.

Contracts for commercial items differ from the usual government contracts in the method provided for acceptance of product. While in most situations the government will inspect a shipment prior to its leaving the contractor's facility, usually by a person designated a "Quality Assurance Representative" (QAR), in the case of a contract for commercial items, the government will rely on the contractor's quality system, although it will inspect a shipment once it arrives at the destination and it reserves the right to perform inspections at the contractor's facility.

SIMPLIFIED ACQUISITIONS (FAR PART 13)

FAR Subpart 13 prescribes the procedures to be followed when a contract is expected to be below the Simplified Acquisition Threshold (SAT), currently $150,000. The purpose of Simplified Acquisition procedures is to reduce government administrative costs while at the same time improving opportunities for small, small disadvantaged, woman-owned, veteran-owned, and HUBZone firms to obtain a fair proportion of government contracts.

In acquisitions below the micro threshold of $3,000, agencies are permitted to use informal procedures, such as verbally soliciting vendors. Even in such cases, contracting officers are expected to solicit as many potential offerors as possible. A firm that wants to participate in these micro acquisitions would be smart to market its capabilities to agencies that might be expected to buy that firm's products or services, so that the firm will be contacted when opportunities arise. In addition to the government's System For

Award Management (SAM), agencies are permitted to maintain their own vendor files and source lists.

In procurements that exceed the $3,000 micro threshold but do not exceed the Simplified Acquisition threshold, the preferred method for conducting the procurement is by Request for Quotations (RFQ). While competitions conducted by way of RFQs may use procedures usually applicable to sealed bidding or negotiated acquisitions (such as the use of technical evaluation factors), quotations submitted in response to a RFQ are not offers. Quotations are considered "informational," meaning the government does not award a contract in response to a quotation. If a quotation is selected, the contracting officer sends the offeror a purchase order for signature. When the purchase order is signed by the offeror, the contract is formed. An offeror is free, however, to decline to sign the purchase order in the event the offeror no longer wants the contract. In the case of micro purchases, the contracting officer will simply send out an order. When the seller ships the product, formation of the contract is complete.

One of the methods authorized for fulfilling acquisitions under the SAT is by use of Blanket Purchase Agreements (BPA). A BPA is not a contract. It is simply the establishment of a price list between the government and a contractor, delineating the types of goods or services the contractor can supply and the prices it will charge. The government is not committing to purchase any particular item or service or any particular quantity. Even in the case of an acquisition by way of BPAs, contracting officers are to maximize competition by soliciting several firms that hold BPAs for a given item or service.

If there are not a sufficient number of BPAs to conduct a competition, other small businesses are to be solicited.

Sealed Bidding (FAR Part 14)

Sealed bidding is the method most people probably think of when they think of government competitions. In sealed bidding, the government specifies a due date and time when all bids will be opened in public, meaning bidders are free to attend and watch the bids being opened. While attendance at a bid opening is not required, it can be advantageous. Once the contracting officer opens and reads the bids, anyone present is free to inspect them. In some cases a bidder may find that the bidder who has just beaten them out on the price has failed to acknowledge a material amendment or has somehow qualified its bid, making it non-responsive. In that event, the bid must be rejected. Another common mistake made in construction procurements is an improper bid bond or payment bond. Photocopied signatures, for example, are not permitted, and the bond must be in the proper amount. Bid bonds are generally required to be in amount sufficient to cover the base work and all priced options. I have seen many situations where bidders submit bid bonds in the amount of the base bid when the solicitation required the bonds to be in amount sufficient to cover the base work plus all options that the government might choose to add. In that case there can be no post-bid opening correction, and the bid must be rejected. The lesson to take from this is that a bidder should not depend on the government people to exclude a non-responsive bid; deficiencies can easily be missed. If you are not the winning bidder and it is at all possible, get a look at the winner's bid.

Solicitations in competitions conducted by sealed bidding do not include evaluation factors. While they may include certain requirements in terms of experience or perhaps a license requirement, in the case of sealed bidding these go to the bidder's "responsibility." The bid consists simply of a filled-out bid form. In the case of sealed bidding, unlike negotiated acquisitions, there are no exchanges between the government and the bidders. There is only the review of the bids to determine responsiveness and, in the case of the lowest bidder, responsibility. If the bidder with the lowest responsive bid is found to be non-responsible, the government moves to the next higher bidder to determine if that bidder is responsible. The contract then goes to the lowest responsive, responsible bidder.

The rule in government contracting is that all bidders are presumed to be non-responsible. It is up to the bidder to demonstrate that it is responsible. Generally this is done by way of a pre-award survey during which government personnel such as financial analysts and industrial specialists review every aspect of the proposed awardee's operation to determine whether the firm has the "capacity and credit" (meaning ability and financing) to perform the contract.

As noted above, in the case of sealed bidding the award goes to the lowest bidder so long as its bid is responsive and its has been determined to be responsible. If the low bid has been rejected for responsibility reasons (but not for responsiveness reasons) and the bidder is a small business, it has the right to appeal the determination to the Small Business

Administration (SBA) for possible issuance of a Certificate of Competency (COC). See Chapter 4, Socioeconomic Programs. If SBA issues a COC, the contracting officer must award that bidder the contract.

Contracting by Negotiation (FAR Part 15)

Perhaps no single contracting method used by the government has spawned the amount of protest litigation as has contracting by negotiation. The concept was simple in principle: having to award the contract to the lowest bidder (as is the case in publicly-opened bids) can be false economy, since the lowest bidder may be a company that is desperate for work and bids a price below what is required to perform the contract. Terminating the awardee for default later does no one any good. Contracting by negotiation was meant to remedy that by allowing for the government to give equal or greater weight than price to technical factors such as performance history.

The problem is that in publicly-opened bids, evaluations are somewhat objective, meaning that the lowest bidder can be readily determined. In contracting by negotiation, technical evaluations are by nature subjective. The quality and relevance of a company's experience are often in the eye of the beholder, and in many cases an offeror who sees the award go to another offeror at a higher price will feel compelled to challenge the decision by way of a protest.

The major advantage in contracting by negotiation over sealed bidding is that it allows the government to engage in exchanges with offerors in an effort to enhance each offeror's chance of winning the contract. Exchanges may involve asking an offeror questions so the government can better understand the technical proposal. Those exchanges are referred to as "clarifications." When the government advises an offeror of deficiencies and/or weaknesses in a technical proposal and allows the offeror an opportunity to address these deficiencies or weaknesses by revising the proposal, the exchanges are called "discussions."

The distinction between clarifications and discussions has in and of itself been the cause of much protest litigation. As will be discussed below, the government need not engage in clarifications with all offerors, but if it engages in discussions with one offeror, it must engage in discussions with all the offerors. Moreover, all offerors must then be allowed to revise their proposal. Disagreements over whether the government has engaged in discussions or clarifications with the awardee are often resolved in a protest.

Lowest Price Technically Acceptable Versus Best Value Methodologies

There are two main methodologies used in negotiated competitions: Lowest Price Technically Acceptable ("LPTA") and Best Value. In LPTA, the award decision is similar to the decision in sealed bidding: the contract award goes to the technically-acceptable offeror who has submitted the lowest price. The difference between LPTA methodology and sealed bidding is that the government may engage in clarifications and/or discussions with offerors to determine who the technically acceptable offerors are. An offeror who is initially found to be technically unacceptable may yet receive the award if it can cure the unacceptability as a result of discussions.

In "Best Value" methodology, the government evaluates the offerors comparatively, meaning against each other, by weighing technical capability and price. In Best Value methodology, the solicitation will specify how much weight will be given to price, i.e., equal to the technical factors, less important than technical factors, or significantly less important than technical factors.

As with LPTA, in Best Value procurements the government may engage in clarifications and/or discussions aimed at determining which offerors are the highest technically-rated. At the end of that process, the offerors are ranked. If the offeror with the highest technical rating has the lowest price there is no issue; that offeror receives the award. What if the offeror with the highest technical ranking is not the lowest priced? Then the Source Selection Authority (SSA) charged with selecting the awardee evaluates the offers by way of a trade-off process aimed at determining whether the technical superiority of a highly rated offeror justifies paying a higher price. In other words, the SSA must determine whether the government should pay for a Cadillac when a Chevrolet can do the job.

Competitors in a procurement using the Best Value methodology must pay particular attention to how the technical evaluation factors are weighted versus price or cost. Price or cost must be evaluated in every competition, even if technical factors are significantly more important. An offeror lacking a past performance history, so as to require a "neutral" rating for past performance, may be able to overcome it by offering a particularly low price. Essentially, a new company may have to operate with little or no profit until it is able to establish a track record of top-level performance so as to allow it to offer higher prices "down the road" and still be found to be the Best Value.

Evaluation Factors in Negotiated Solicitations

The FAR gives agencies wide leeway in choosing technical evaluations factors. Past performance must be an evaluation factor in all negotiated procurements unless the contracting officer makes a specific finding as to why evaluation of the offerors' past performance is not appropriate for the particular competition. What if an offeror has no record of past performance? How is that offeror to be evaluated? The FAR states that in the case of an offeror with no record of past performance, the offeror will receive a "neutral" rating; neither favorable nor unfavorable.

In service contracts, agencies will generally evaluate information on the qualifications of an offeror's key employees by requiring resumes. Another common evaluation factor in service contracts is the offeror's transition plan; both transitioning into the contract at the beginning and out of it at the other end if the offeror does not win the contract again when it is next competed. In competitions for supply contracts, agencies may require product samples for evaluation against the government's specification. Regardless of what the technical evaluation factors are, and regardless of how they are weighted, price or cost must be a factor in every competition, no matter whether conducted using sealed bidding or negotiated procedures.

While price or cost must be a factor in all procurements, only cost reasonableness must be considered in every award decision. "Reasonableness" refers to whether the offered price is too high. The government cannot award a contract at a price that is too high, and the contracting officer must determine that the price is "reasonable" before awarding a contract. Price or cost "realism" refers to an offered price being too low. In the case where a firm, fixed-price contract is to be awarded, there is no prohibition on the government awarding a contract at a price that is unrealistically low, even one that is below cost (except in the case of an offeror who is seeking to "buy-in"; see Chapter 3, Contractor Ethics Requirements). Thus there is no requirement that the contracting officer consider price realism in determining to award a firm, fixed-price contract to an offeror. Price realism can be considered, though, in a firm, fixed-price contract competition where the solicitation called for it to be considered as part of the evaluation process to determine whether an offeror fully understands the requirements of the solicitation.

Cost reimbursement contracts are a wholly different matter, though. Since the government will be required to reimburse the contractor its actual costs, it gains the government no benefit to award the contract to an offeror that has "low-balled" its estimate and will end up billing far more hours than its original estimate called for. Therefore, cost or price "realism" is a mandatory factor in all solicitations that contemplate the award of a cost reimbursement-type contract. It is interesting to note that the distinction between "realism" and "reasonableness" is often not understood, even among government cost and price analysts. I participated in a GAO protest hearing not long ago and heard a government price analyst with many years of experience testify that in his mind price "realism" and price "reasonableness" meant the same thing.

Evaluating Price of Cost

How price or cost is evaluated, according to the GAO, is largely up to the agency. One common method is for the agency to describe the work and have the offerors submit cost estimates. Agency evaluators, generally working with an "Independent Government Cost Estimate" (IGCE), then evaluate whether an offeror has included enough hours to perform the described work. Additionally, the evaluators check the offerors' proposed hourly rates for the different job descriptions to ensure the offeror will not be under-paying the employees, for that raises concerns as to whether the contractor will be able to hire and retain qualified personnel. Another method for evaluating an offeror's cost-estimating ability is by use of a sample task. A sample task will often require the offerors to price different types of work and provide indirect expense rates to measure against the government's own estimate for the sample task.

As we mentioned above, how cost is evaluated is left to each agency, according to the GAO. However, whatever method is chosen, it must bear some relation to the costs to be billed in the resultant contract. Some years ago, an agency proposed to award multi-award renovation contracts. The solicitation called for cost to be evaluated by having the offerors simply state their proposed indirect rates (i.e., overhead and G&A expense), which would then become part of the contract. Our office protested successfully to the GAO that such an evaluation scheme would provide no illumination on a contractor's cost structure. An offeror could propose low indirect rates for the contract, and then make up the short-fall by simply applying a "fudge-factor" (say 25 percent, for example) to proposed direct costs when it came time to price an actual project.

Establishing a Competitive Range

One tool in contracting by negotiation that the government uses frequently is the establishment of a competitive range. Essentially this allows the government to "cull the herd," by eliminating offerors who have little chance of receiving the award prior to engaging in discussions with the remaining offerors. This reduces the number of offerors with whom discussions are to be conducted and who have to be evaluated in the final award decision. A competitive range is a fluid thing. As a competition moves along, offerors who are in the competitive range may later be removed if after discussions they no longer have a realistic chance of receiving the award.

In establishing a competitive range the government evaluates all offerors, basing the evaluation on initial proposals. Then, per FAR 15.306(c)(2), the government ranks the proposals and establishes a competitive range comprised of the "most highly rated proposals." This does not mean the proposals that are the most highly rated technically, since price must always be considered in evaluations. In the initial evaluations, offerors are ranked based on the weighing of technical factors and price as set out in the solicitation. The offerors who have no realistic chance of receiving the award, whether due to low technical ratings or high price, or a combination of both, are excluded from the competitive range. They are then notified that they have been excluded from the competitive range and eliminated from further participation in the competition. There is, however, one requirement for the government to communicate with offerors before the establishment of the competitive range. If an offeror's past performance record is the determining factor preventing that offeror from being included in the competitive range, FAR 15.306(b) requires that the contracting officer engage in "communications" with that offeror to provide it an opportunity to address the negative past performance information.

If you receive notification that you have been eliminated from the competitive range, that does not necessarily mean you had a poor proposal or an unreasonably high price. It may be a reflection of how many highly-rated offerors there were or how many offerors were willing to submit extremely low prices in the hope of receiving the award.

The Conduct of Negotiations

"Negotiations" are exchanges between the government and offerors after the establishment of a competitive range. If, as noted above, the "negotiations" involve having offerors address weaknesses or deficiencies in their proposals, the negotiations are referred to as "Discussions." Discussions take place in negotiated procurements only. The primary purpose of discussions is to maximize the government's ability to obtain best value for its money.

The question is often asked, "Must the government conduct discussions in every procurement conducted using negotiated procedures?" The answer is that an award may be made without discussions if the solicitation contained a notice that the government intended to make the award without discussions, but advising offerors that the government reserves the right to conduct discussions if the contracting officer decides discussions are necessary. What offerors will see in many solicitations is the notice that the government intends to make the award without discussions, even if that is not actually the intent. By including the notice in a solicitation, the government can wait until it sees the offers before deciding whether to conduct discussions. If the government does choose to conduct discussions, it must do so with every offeror who is in the competitive range.

There are strict rules regarding the content of discussions. FAR 15.306 requires that discussions must be tailored to each individual offeror. The contracting officer must discuss with each offeror deficiencies and significant weaknesses in its proposal. Adverse past performance information to which the offeror has not had the opportunity to respond previously must also be raised so that the offeror has an opportunity to respond. Discussions must be "meaningful." They must lead an offeror into the areas that the government perceives as deficiencies or significant weaknesses in the proposal. In 15.306(e), the FAR delineates what the contracting officer cannot do during discussions. The contracting officer may not:

1. favor one offeror over another;

2. reveal any proprietary information regarding one offeror to another;

3. reveal another offeror's price (although an offeror may be told the government considers its price to be too high);

4. reveal the names of persons providing reference information; or

5. knowingly reveal source selection information.

As mentioned above, discussions are markedly different than clarifications. Clarifications are limited exchanges between the government and offerors that may occur when the award is to be made without discussions, and they need not be conducted with every offeror. During clarifications, an offeror may be given the opportunity to explain certain aspects of its proposal, such as the relevance of past performance information or adverse past performance information. However, an offeror will not be permitted to revise its proposal, because it is the opportunity to revise a proposal that distinguishes discussions from clarifications. A technically deficient proposal cannot be corrected in the course of clarifications. The "clarifications" versus "discussions" conflict has been the cause of much protest litigation, as unsuccessful offerors have claimed that the successful competitor was afforded the opportunity for discussions while they were not. What the contracting officer calls the exchange is not determinative. If the awardee, under the guise of clarifications, was allowed to submit what is effectively a revised proposal, then the exchange amounted to discussions and every other offeror should have had the same opportunity.

Final Proposal Revisions

Once discussions are concluded, each offeror still in the Competitive Range must be given an opportunity to submit a Final Proposal Revision (FPR), essentially what was formerly known as a Best and Final Offer (BAFO). Even offerors who were not afforded the opportunity for discussions (because the government found no deficiencies or significant weaknesses in their proposals to discuss) are to be given the opportunity to submit an FPR. When submitting an FPR, offerors are not limited to revising their prices or the areas in the proposal that the government raised during discussions. An offeror can revise any aspect of its proposal that it believes can enhance the chances of receiving the award. It is also important to keep in mind that the rules regarding late bids apply to FPRs. A late FPR cannot be considered by the government.

Offerors should be aware that submission of FPRs may not be the end of the exchanges. Discussions may be reopened after FPRs if the government deems it necessary, but in that event, the government must afford all offerors still in the competitive range the opportunity for reopened discussions. Where the government reevaluates proposals after discussions are complete and identifies a new deficiency in an offeror's proposal, discussions must be reopened. However, the government is not required to bring up in a second round of discussions deficiencies that remain in an offeror's initial proposal and which were brought up in the first round of discussions. If discussions are reopened after FPRs and a contractor is still in the competitive range, it will have the opportunity to submit a new FPR. Once all FPRs have been evaluated, the award will be made.

Online Reverse Auctions

In recent years the government has added online reverse auctions to its arsenal of techniques in contracting by negotiation. How it works is fairly simple in principle. Assuming the solicitation provided the option for use of an online reverse auction following the conclusion of discussions, those offerors still in the competitive range are invited to participate in the auction. The lowest offered price is posted as a starting point. The participating offerors, all of whom are anonymous, are then permitted (encouraged is perhaps more descriptive) to offer pricing below that which has been posted. When new, lower pricing is offered, that new pricing appears and becomes the new "target." Generally, online auctions run for thirty minutes, at which time the auction automatically closes and the low price is established.

The inherent problem with the online reverse auction technique stems from its use in negotiated acquisitions applying the "Best Value" source selection technique. Under "Best Value," as I discussed above, the government may bypass the lowest-price offeror in favor of a higher-priced offeror with a better performance record. Since "Best Value" techniques require a cost versus technical capability trade-off, in theory an offeror with a spotty track record can still win the contract by offering a very low price. Thus in a reverse auction, the offeror driving the prices down may well be an offeror with a poor performance record. In the end, when the government performs the final cost versus technical capability trade-off, that offeror may still not receive the contract. Yet, that offeror is the one that forced the other, more quali-fied offerors to reduce their prices substantially. Thus, if the goal is for the government to get the cheapest possible price without regard to the detriment to the continued viability of qualified small businesses, the online reverse auction is a valuable tool. Of course the government could achieve the same result simply by eliminating small busi-ness set-asides and acquiring all of its products and services from mega businesses.

Debriefings

Unique to contracting by negotiating is the opportunity for offerors to receive a debriefing, outlining how their proposals were evaluated. An offeror that receives notification that it has been eliminated from the competitive range should be sure to request a debriefing. Anything that can be learned may help the offeror's chances in the next competition. Whether an offeror receives its debriefing immediately (referred to as a pre-award debriefing) or after the name of the awardee is announced (a post-award debriefing) is up to the offeror. I recommend that offerors request the pre-award debriefing. The offeror may learn that there was a mistake in the evaluation of its proposal, such that the agency may opt to restore that offeror to the competition. If the excluded offeror waits until after the award and then learns of the mistake, it will be too late to do anything about it (see Chapter 9, Contract Awards and Competition Controversies). Additionally, if the offeror is restored to the competition, what was learned during the debriefing may enhance the offeror's ability to win the award by steering it toward where to make revisions to the proposal during the discussions process. Finally, an offeror should always request a debriefing, even if it is the one who received the award. Anything that can be learned is of value.

Competitions Among Federal Supply Schedule Contractors

An agency is not required to undertake a competition before issuing a purchase order to a Federal Supply Schedule (FSS) contractor, because the award of the original FSS contract is considered to be the equivalent of a competitive award. Most contracting officers, though, will request quotes from several FSS contractors to determine whether one of the FSS contractors will offer a discount on its schedule pricing. In some cases, contracting officers will conduct a full-fledged competition limited to FSS holders, using the techniques in FAR Part 15 for negotiated contracts. In such competitions only those FSS contract holders with the particular item or service on their FSS contract list can compete. An order to an FSS contractor cannot include an item or service that is not on that FSS contractor's item list (even if that contractor would be able to supply it).

SOLE-SOURCE AND LIMITED-SOURCE PROCUREMENTS

CICA authorizes contracting officers to make awards without competition when there is only one source available to satisfy the government's need, such as a maintenance contract to service a particular company's computers. Whenever the government intends to make such a sole-source award, it must publish a notice on FedBizOps. The notice is not an invitation for bids or a request for proposals, rather it is meant to alert other potential sources to the government's need and give them the opportunity to demonstrate that they can satisfy that need. Even in the case of a sole-source procurement, CICA mandates that agencies at least try and identify opportunities for competition.

Similar to sole-source awards are situations where the agency decides to limit the pool of expected offerors. Most often, these restricted competition situations arise where logistics issues suggest limiting offers to potential sources located within a certain state or a certain geographic area. Contracts for emergency hurricane clean-up efforts are most often the types of situations where such limitations are used, since time does not allow for contractors from far away to "gear up" for performance. In some situations the government may limit offers to potential sources with specific specialized experience so as not to waste the government's time or the offerors' time evaluating proposals from offerors who have no hope of receiving the award. So long as the restriction is reasonably related to the agency's requirements, a protest against the restriction will be denied.

MANDATORY SOURCES

There are a number of sources for products and services designated as "mandatory" under federal law. One is the Committee For Purchase From People Who Are Blind Or Severely Disabled ("the Committee"), currently referred to as "AbilityOne." Under the Javits-Wagner-O'Day Act, it is federal policy to procure a certain percentage of goods and services from non-profit agencies that employ such persons. The Committee makes determinations as to which goods or services procured by a federal agency are appropriate for inclusion in the program. The Committee then adds the item or service to its Procurement List, negotiates a "fair market price" with the federal agency, and allocates the contract to one of its participating non-profit contractors at that fair market price. Another such mandatory source is Federal Prison Industries (FPI), also known as "UNICOR," which is a wholly government-owned corporation that enters into contracts with procuring agencies to provide work to federal prisoners.

Why should these mandatory sources be of interest to small business contractors? They can affect a small company's business in a big way. In the case of AbilityOne, the Committee has the right to take a product or service being procured competitively by a federal agency (or a certain percentage of those products or services), and add it to the Committee's procurement list for allocation to its non-profit agencies. Once an item or service is added to the list, it is no longer available for competition amongst for-profit contractors; only a non-profit participant in the program can receive the contract. Before an item is added to the Committee's procurement list, the Committee must publish a notice and also attempt to notify small businesses who may have supplied the item or service in the recent past, so as to allow them to argue against the addition to the product list on the basis of the adverse effect. For a small business contractor, receiving such a notice can have serious consequences.

In the case of FPI, it maintains a Procurement List similar to the Committee. There is one significant difference, though: federal law allows FPI, which pays its inmates eleven ($0.11) cents per hour, to submit bids or offers on competitive procurements, including small business set-asides. Agencies are allowed some discretion in awarding such competitive contracts to FPI, but a small business may find itself competing with FPI for a contract on some occasion.

Special Procedures for Use in Contracting for Construction (FAR Subpart 36)

FAR Subpart 36.2 lays out special rules and procedures for use in competitions for construction contracts. First, an advance notice must be posted on FedBizOps, providing an estimate of the magnitude of the project:

    (a) less than $25,000

    (b) between $25,000 and $100,000

    (c) between $100,000 and $250,000

    (d) between $250,000 and $500,000

    (e) between $500,000 and $1,000,000

    (f) between $1,000,000 and $5,000,000

(g) between $5,000,000 and $10,000,000

(h) over $10,000,000

The requirement makes sense. No one wants to see small companies waste their time pursing contracts far above anything they could ever hope to perform. In addition, agencies are to make arrangements to allow prospective offerors an opportunity to inspect the project site and to examine any site data available to the government. Another requirement applicable to competitions for construction contracts involves liquidated damages clauses. FAR 36.206 requires that contracting officers evaluate the need for inclusion of a liquidated damages provision in all solicitations for construction contracts.

As a general rule, firm, fixed-price contracts are used for construction projects, except that a fixed-price contract with Economic Price Adjustment (EPA) can be used where such a clause is common for that type of project or where the omission of an EPA clause would preclude a significant number of offerors from competing or would result in offerors including unwarranted contingencies in their prices.

The two-phase design-build method for conducting acquisitions is appropriate for use, according to FAR 36.301(b), where the agency anticipates receiving at least three offers, and the project's design work must be performed by offerors prior to being able to prepare price or cost proposals, thereby incurring a "substantial" amount of cost. In such a case the solicitation will provide procedures for a Phase One competition, including technical evaluation factors for both Phase One and Phase Two, and a statement of how many offers will be selected to compete in Phase Two. Cost or price is not a factor in the Phase One competition. Generally the Phase Two competitors will be limited to five (5), unless the contracting officer decides that for the particular solicitation more than five (5) Phase Two offerors is in the government's best interest. The Phase Two solicitation will then require submission of technical and price proposals for evaluation leading up to the award.

Conclusion

As you can see, there are significant differences between the various methods the government uses to conduct its competitions and you will need to have a basic understanding of those differences, such as those between publicly-opened bids and competitive proposals, or between "Lowest Price Technically Acceptable" and "Best Value" evaluation schemes. Those distinctions will determine how you structure your bid or proposal and whether you will have an opportunity to revise your proposal or your price during the competition (such as with competitive proposals) or whether there will be one unchangeable submission (as with publicly-opened bids). Losing a contract because you did not know the rules before you entered the game will leave you kicking yourself for months.

Chapter 7

TYPES OF CONTRACTS

T here are a number of different contract vehicles that form the basis of contracting with the federal government. It is extremely important when you are bidding on a government contract that you understand exactly what kind of contract the government is planning on issuing, for a misunderstanding on your part can have dire consequences. Some contracts, such as firm, fixed-price contracts, contain no mechanism to increase the price in the event that performance costs are increased through no fault of your own. Other types of contracts provide for price adjustments when the contractor experiences cost increases.

FIRM, FIXED-PRICE (FFP) CONTRACTS

By far the most common type of contract utilized by the government, especially in the case of a small business providing manufactured products, is the firm, fixed-price (FFP) contract. As the name describes, the contract calls for the government to pay a set price for the product it is buying. Despite what the media may frequently report about huge cost overruns on government contracts (most of which are on major weapons development contracts), FFP contracts have no provision by which the contractor can receive an increase in the contract price. Therefore, even though a contractor may have experienced an increase in the cost of performing, such as an increase in the federal minimum wage or a dramatic increase in the cost of a necessary component, there is no vehicle in the contract for the contractor to be paid anything more than the price set by the contract. It is immaterial that the cost increase may have been unforeseen, such as the Arab oil embargo in the 1970s, or even a Congressionally-mandated increase in the minimum wage. The risk in a FFP contract is all on the contractor. This is true even where the solicitation requires a bidder to offer prices on government options as much as four (4) years or more (given the time necessary to make an award) down the road from when the bid was submitted. It behooves bidders to try and protect themselves against contingencies when a price on options several years out must be offered. While doing so may mean losing the contract, that seems preferable to winning the contract and then going out of business.

The only exception to the foregoing rule is the doctrine in contract law of "commercial impracticability," which is applicable to government contracts as it is to commercial contracts. The doctrine will not get a contractor more money, but it may get the contractor out of the contract. Basically that doctrine holds that when the cost or performance on a contract increases to the point where continued performance could cause the contractor to go out of business, performance may be excused. To fall within this rule, though, the cost increase must be truly gargantuan. Increases of 50 percent or even 90 percent in the cost of performance may not suffice, especially if the contractor has other contracts on which it is not losing money, since those contracts can absorb the losses on the contract in question. While the doctrine of "commercial impracticability" is available to government contractors, they should not rely on it saving them, especially if the problem arises from aggressive pricing in the original bid or offer.

Firm, Fixed-Price with Economic Price Adjustment (EPA)

The government does recognize that certain items and services it buys often require the contractor to utilize components for which the market can be volatile. Examples include leather or aluminum. In such cases the solicitation will often include an Economic Price Adjustment (EPA) clause providing for adjustments in the contract price. Adjustments, in accordance with FAR 16.203-1, may be based on: (1) established prices, (2) actual costs, and (3) cost indexes of labor and material. In the case of the first method, the contractor certifies that the prices in the contract's schedule are not in excess of its established market prices. If those established market prices are increased during the life of the contract, the contractor may request a corresponding increase in the contract's price schedule. However, the limit on such upward adjustments is 10 percent of the contract price in the aggregate.

The second type of EPA is one based on increases in the cost of labor or materials. In this case, the contract clause will specify the specific types of labor and material subject to adjustment. The contractor may request an adjustment due to increases in the cost of the specific labor or material, which request is subject to audit by the government. After audit the contractor and the contracting officer will attempt to negotiate the actual increase.

The third type of EPA is one tied to one of the recognized indexes, such as the Producer Price Index, the Employment Cost Index, or the Wage and Income Series by Standard Classification (Labor). Generally, adjustment clauses based on an established index do not include a ceiling or floor limiting the adjustments. When reviewing a solicitation for possible submission of a bid, a potential bidder should review it carefully to determine if it contains an EPA clause, and if so, what method is established. Bidders should be aware, though, that an EPA clause works both ways: it can result in a price reduction if the specified government index were to show a reduction.

FIXED-PRICE REDERTERMINABLE CONTRACTS

This type of contract is no longer commonly used since it does not provide incentive for the contractor to control costs. In the first type, fixed-price with prospective redetermination (FAR 16.205), a fixed price is established for a base period, where it is not possible to project the cost of the goods or services. Subsequent periods are subject to establishment of prices going forward based on the base period experience.

In the second type, fixed-price with retroactive determination (appropriate for research and development contracts under the Simplified Acquisition Threshold, per FAR 16.206), a fixed-ceiling price contract is established at the outset. After completion of the work, the final price is negotiated. Since this type of contract clearly provides no incentive on the contractor to control costs, the ceiling price is to provide for some sharing of the risk by the contractor. Additionally, the contracting officer is required to make clear to the contractor during negotiations before award that its "management effectiveness and ingenuity" will be considered in arriving at the final price.

Cost Reimbursement Contracts

In cost reimbursement contracts, exclusively used in contracts for services, the bidder proposes hourly rates for various types of employees. Those rates are usually "burdened" rates, meaning the contractor has included its overhead, general and administrative (G&A) expense, and profit in the hourly rates. Then, as contract performance proceeds, the contractor bills its employees' time at the contract's specified rates and the contractor is "reimbursed" those costs. Cost reimbursement contracts are generally used in the case of service contracts where the government is unsure initially of the type and amount of the services it will require. Before seeing dollar signs dancing before their eyes, offerors should bear in mind that in cost reimbursement contracts, only costs that are "allowable" and "allocable" may be billed to the government. Entire books have been written on those two subjects and I do not have the space to cover them in depth. I will cover them in Chapter 12, Getting Paid.

There are two types of cost-reimbursement contracts: the basic cost plus fixed-fee (CPFF) contract and the incentive type, which may be cost plus incentive fee (CPIF) or cost plus award fee (CPAF). We will discuss them in turn.

Cost Plus Fixed-Fee (CPFF) Contracts

In a CPFF contract, the contractor and the government negotiate an estimated cost to perform the work and establish a set fee, in dollars, that the contractor will receive for performing the work. The contractor will receive its actual costs of performing the work stated in the contract, and the risk of the fee's adequacy is on the contractor. However, if additional work not contemplated in the contract is required to complete performance, then the fee will be adjusted, so the government then bears the risk of additional cost to complete the work.

Incentive Contracts

In CPIF and CPAF contracts, the government reimburses the cost for the contractor's employees' work. In the case of a CPIF contract, the contract will include a formula to determine the amount of profit based on the contractor's actual performance. A CPIF contract will usually include a target cost, a target fee, minimum and maximum fees, and a formula for determining the final fee. The formula will provide increases in the target fee when actual performance costs are lower than the target costs. The final fee will then be determined once performance is complete by use of the formula. A CPIF type contract, then, is a contract in which the fee is determined "objectively" (by use of the formula). A CPAF contract, on the other hand, provides for determination of the contractor's fee in a "subjective" manner. The contract will provide for a base fee fixed at the time of contracting (say 4 percent of costs), and for an additional award fee that the contractor can earn based on the agency's judgment as to the quality of its performance measured against the criteria stated in the contract (0 percent up to 4 percent, for example).

INDEFINITE DELIVERY CONTRACTS

Indefinite delivery contracts give the government flexibility when its needs, in terms of quantities or deliveries, cannot be readily forecasted. There are two basic types of indefinite delivery contracts: Indefinite Delivery/Indefinite Quantity (IDIQ) contracts and Requirements contracts. It is important to understand the key distinction between them.

This type of contract is used when the government is unaware of what quantity of goods or services it may require and/or when it will require them. In an IDIQ contract the government specifies a guaranteed minimum quantity that it promises to purchase and a maximum quantity that it may purchase. Regardless of any estimates in the solicitation as to what the government expects to order, the contractor is not guaranteed any amount above the stated minimum. It is the guarantee of a stated minimum purchase that forms the consideration necessary for a contract. While the stated minimum is supposed to be more than a "nominal" quantity, stated minimums I have seen are very often nominal or even less. It is important to understand that in the case of an IDIQ, the government is purchasing the contractor's availability for the stated contractual period to produce the supplies when and if the government needs them. The government can order the minimum immediately, leaving the contractor to remain available for subsequent orders that may never come, or it may wait until the end of the period to place an order for the minimum quantity. So long as the government has purchased the minimum quantity specified, it has fulfilled the terms of the IDIQ contract, and it is free to purchase the same item or service from another contractor without being in breach of the IDIQ contract.

A requirements contract, also used when the government is unsure of its needs, differs from an IDIQ contract in two major respects. First, there is no guaranteed minimum, i.e., the government is not promising to purchase anything. Estimates or expectations as to what quantities might be purchased that may be provided in the solicitation are of little consequence and bidders cannot rely on them. The only requirement for a government estimate in a competition for a "requirements" contract is that it be a "good faith" estimate. For example, an estimate that states the government expects to order a hundred thousand monitors is not a good faith estimate when the contracting officer knows that need for the item has disappeared and no more than a thousand will be ordered.

Second, in exchange for the lack of a guaranteed minimum quantity, what the government does promise in a requirements contract is that it will satisfy all of its "require-ments" for the particular item or service by ordering from the contractor. This promise forms the consideration for a con-tract. In other words, in a solicitation for a requirements contract, the government is saying, "We are not promising we will order any of these, but if we do order them, we will order them from you."

JOB ORDER, TASK ORDER, OR DELIVERY ORDER CONTRACTS

Another type of IDIQ contracting mainly used in the area of construction is the job order or task order type contract. Such a contract is defined in the FAR as "a contract for services that does not procure or specify a firm quantity of services (other than a minimum or maximum quantity) and that provides for the issuance of orders for the performance of tasks during the period of the contract." One type of task order contract is the multiple award task order contract (MATOC), while the other is the single award task order contract (SATOC). In a MATOC, the government awards IDIQ contracts for facility design, construction, or maintenance services that are required on a recurring basis to a number of contractors, usually five to ten. Each contractor is guaranteed a small amount of work over the life of the contract. However, most projects or orders for services are awarded as task orders by way of competitions amongst all the contractors. Essentially, a MATOC is a way for the government to establish a group of qualified contractors for future competitions so as to avoid having to evaluate dozens of proposals every time there is a requirement. In a SATOC, as the name implies, the government awards a single IDIQ contract to one contractor, also for facility design, construction, or maintenance services. The contractor is guaranteed a small amount of work, and additional task orders may then be issued over the life of the contract for additional projects.

Similar to the task order contracts for services are delivery order contracts (DOCs), which the FAR defines as "a contract for supplies that does not procure or specify a firm quantity of services (other than a minimum or maximum quantity) and that provides for the issuance of orders for the delivery of supplies during the period of the contract." Thus, the basic distinction between a DOC and a MATOC or SATOC is that a DOC is for supplies rather than services. A DOC can be either multiple award, in which case several offerors receive contracts for a basic quantity and then compete for subsequent orders, or single award.

GOVERNMENT-WIDE ACQUISITION CONTRACTS

A government-wide acquisition contract (GWAC) is a special version of an IDIQ contract used by the government exclusively for the acquisition of information technology products and services. It is essentially a contract that allows multiple federal agencies to acquire info-technology products and services from the contractor(s).

TIME AND MATERIALS CONTRACTS

Perhaps the simplest type of federal contract is a time and materials (T&M) contract. Under a T&M contract, the government pays the contractor for its employees' time at rates established in the contract. Materials are reimbursed at the contractor's cost. T&M contracts are used in simple construction or renovation jobs.

BLANKET PURCHASE AGREEMENT AND BASIC ORDERING AGREEMENTS

Blanket Purchase Agreements (BPAs) and Basic Ordering Agreements (BOAs) are not actually contracts, because they contain no mutual commitments (i.e., no "consideration"). A BPA or BOA is simply an agreement to establish a price list. The government does not commit to purchasing anything; it will issue orders for a product or service listed in the BPA or BOA when and if it has a need. At that point the "contractor" has the option to accept the order and deliver the product or service, or decline the order without any penalty.

UNDEFINITIZED CONTRACT ACTIONS

In some cases where a particular item may be so new as to not to have a pricing history, or where the government has an urgent need for an item that does not allow the time for the usual cost proposal, audit, and negotiation process, the government may enter into a contract where the final price is not established; the price is "undefinitized." In such a situation the contract will have a billing price for the item, which establishes the ceiling price that the government will pay. As contract performance proceeds, the contractor submits a proposal to set ("definitize") the final price, based on its experience to that point. That proposal is audited, after which the contractor and the contracting officer negotiate the final figure. That final figure is almost certainly going to be less than the ceiling price in the original contract, so a contractor may conceivably owe money back to the government. Negotiation of the final price will be subject to the Truth in Negotiations Act (TINA) requirements (see Chapter 9).

GSA Federal Supply Schedule (FSS) Contracts

If a company markets commercial items or services, the GSA Federal Supply Schedule (FSS) is a good place to be. The FSS is run out of the GSA's Fort Worth, Texas offices. Every year there is an open season during which companies can negotiate long-term contracts directly with the GSA. The negotiations are not competitive; offerors submit their information for GSA's review, and if an offeror is found acceptable, an FSS contract will be issued, listing that offeror's items or services and establishing base pricing. Effectively the FSS contract contains the basic contract terms. Since there is already a contract, an FSS supplier is considered to have already competed for its award. Government buyers can order directly from an FSS contractor without the need for further competition, although in situations where there are multiple FSS sources for an item or service the government will usually initiate a competition limited to those sources. Generally, FSS contracts are for a five-year base period with two (2) additional five-year government option periods, meaning the contract could be as much as fifteen years long.

One interesting quirk about FSS contracting is that a contractor's status is established at the time it enters into the contract. A contractor awarded an FSS contract as a small business remains a small business for purposes of its FSS contract for the life of that contract (as much as fifteen years), regardless of its actual size. There is one caveat, however. In some cases the contracting officer conducting a particular FSS procurement as a small business set-aside will require each of the FSS competitors to recertify that small business status (although there is nothing mandating that he or she do so). Notwithstanding the fact that a contractor's status for its FSS contract says it is a small business, a contractor cannot certify itself as small for an FSS competition if it is no longer in fact small.

Conclusion

To be sure, the government has a number of different contract types that are designed to fit different contracting situations. You need to be aware of how the different types of contracts are interpreted and administered, such as the distinction between an IDIQ contract and a "requirements" contract, lest you find that the contract you thought would provide you with a significant level of business over its term turns out to be nowhere near the amount you were anticipating, and yet you remain obligated to accept such orders as the government chooses to place.

Chapter 8

SUBMITTING A BID OR OFFER

You've found a government requirement for which you want to compete; now it's time to go for it. If the procurement is being conducted by Invitation for Bids (IFB), you will be submitting a "bid." If the procurement is by way of a Request for Proposals (RFP), your submission is an "offer" or "proposal." Finally, if the solicitation is a request for quotes (RFQ), you are submitting a "quote." Government solicitations can be over a hundred pages long, even for what would seem to be a relative simple item or service. Knowing how to navigate your way through them is imperative.

CLAUSES INCLUDED IN FULL AND CLAUSES INCORPORATED BY REFERENCE

Every solicitation will have pages upon pages of government-generated contract clauses. Some are printed out in full text, while others are "incorporated by reference." Some clauses are mandatory, and will be identified as being incorporated. Other clauses are only incorporated if the block in front of the clause is checked, such as like this: [**X**]. However, in the realm of government contracting there is what is known as the "Christian doctrine," named after a decision by the Court of Claims many years ago in a case bearing that name. The Christian doctrine holds that mandatory clauses are deemed included in every government contract, even if they are not checked or printed in full. The termination for convenience clause, giving the government the right to terminate the contract without incurring breach of contract damages, is one example of a clause that is usually held to have been in a contract regardless of whether the block was checked. Additionally, bidders are likely to find that some contracting agencies have a group of standard forms gathered into one document, often called a "master solicitation." A bidder who sees such a reference in a solicitation should make sure to get a copy of that agency's master solicitation. It is critical that you review all clauses that are in a solicitation, however they may be included. It is no defense or excuse to a violation of or failure to comply with a requirement in a clause for the contractor not to have read it.

CERTIFICATIONS AND REPRESENTATIONS

Every solicitation includes multiple certification and representation requirements. Offerors are asked to check blocks laying out their size status (whether you "are" or "are not" a small business), as well as a number of other statuses (service-disabled veteran-owned or HUBZone certified, for two examples). A bidder may be asked to state whether it has been convicted of a crime within a certain time period prior to the bid, or whether it is delinquent in paying its taxes. The list is long. Offerors should keep in mind that when signing an offer, they are certifying to the truth of every statement and certification they have made in it. It is a felony under federal law to make a false statement to the government (18 U.S.C. § 1001), punishable by a large fine and imprisonment for up to five (5) years.

One representation that is required by most solicitations is a representation that the price includes all applicable state and local taxes. Bidders will want to consult with an attorney knowledgeable on the applicability of state and local taxes to government contractors. Discovering after having received the contract award that there is a state or local tax that the offered price did not provide for is not a basis for a price increase. Another representation common in construction contracts is contained in the clause at FAR 52.236-3, "Site Investigation and Conditions Affecting the Work." This clause states that by submitting a bid the contractor is attesting that it was given the opportunity to visit the site, undertook such investigation as it thought appropriate, and satisfied itself as to the conditions there. This is designed to minimize the government's liability for "Differing Site Conditions" claims (see Chapter 11, Contract Performance Issues).

Government-Provided Specifications

In a competition for a product, other than a COTS (commercial off-the-shelf) item, the solicitation will include some form of specification, also sometimes called a "purchase description." There are two types of government specifications: "design" and "performance." The implications of each could not be more distinct, making it critical that an offeror know the difference. A "design" specification is one in which the government tells the contractor exactly how to make the product by providing a list of operations. Such a specification comes with an implied (but very real) warranty: if the contractor follows the step-by-step instructions in the specification precisely (as it is required to), the result will be an acceptable (and safe) product. If for some reason the result is not an acceptable product, the responsibility falls on the government, as the source of the specification. This is referred to the "Spearin doctrine," after a 1918 U.S. Supreme Court decision. However, to have the protection of that warranty, the contractor must follow the specification's instructions to the letter. Even where a contractor may believe it knows a better way, deviating from the specification's instructions means there is no longer an implied warranty and the contractor "owns" the result. With a "performance" specification, though, there is no warranty, implied or otherwise. The government specifies the result it wants by way of performance standards describing how the product must perform. It is up to the contractor to figure out the manufacturing steps that are required to produce the desired result. In some cases, government specifications have both design and performance aspects. In such a case the implied warranty will attach to the design portion only.

Occasionally, the government does not provide any specification, electing instead to specify a specific manufacturer's product. Such specifications are referred to as "brand name or equal." In a "brand name or equal" procurement, the government identifies a manufacturer's part or model number, together with a list of salient characteristics in that item which the government is seeking. A contractor is free to offer an item other than the brand name one, provided it can show that the item it is offering has those same salient characteristics, so as to be "equal" to the specified item.

If a potential offeror believes there has been a mistake or ambiguity in the government bid package (the solicitation, the statement of work, the specifications, etc.), it must bring this to the attention of the contracting officer prior to bid opening. If a bidder elects to submit a bid relying on its own interpretation, that bidder is assuming the risk that the government's interpretation is the same as its own. If that turns out not to be the case, after the award the bidder may find itself forced into a much more expensive method of performance without any additional compensation. On the other hand, in some cases a mistake or ambiguity may not be obvious. In such a situation, the bidder can rely on its interpretation, so long as that interpretation is reasonable—not necessarily as reasonable as the government's interpretation, but reasonable. That is because mistakes in a bid package, so long as they are not obvious, are construed against the government as the drafter of the package.

Availability of Funds

The government will on occasion issue solicitations and conduct competitions without the funding to pay for performance of the contract that it intends to award. Usually that situation arises near the end of a fiscal year where the contracting agency wants to get a jump-start on a contract to be awarded in the next fiscal year by conducting the competition ahead of time. In that event the solicitation will include the clause at FAR 52.232-1, Availability of Funds. That clause tells bidders that the government does not have the funds available to pay for the work and that any contract award is contingent on the funds becoming available. Unless and until funding becomes available and the contracting officer notifies the contractor in writing, the government has no obligation to pay for any work the contractor does. In the event the funding does not come through, the government can walk away from the contract without owing anything to the contractor.

In Chapter 1, I discussed the authority of contracting officers to enter into contracts, based on the limits in their warrants. Related to that authority are the requirements of the Anti-Deficiency Act (the ADA). Under the ADA, no government official has the authority to authorize or obligate the government to an expenditure of funds that exceeds the funding available in a Congressional appropriation, or to obligate the government to making the expenditure before funding has been appropriated. While there are severe penalties for the government official who violates the ADA, since no government official has authority to enter into a contract in violation of the ADA, it necessarily follows that a contract entered into in violation of the ADA is unenforceable against the government.

The ADA requirements beg the obvious question: how can the government award multi-year contracts with maximum dollar limits in the tens or hundreds of million dollars? It is simple, really. Only the base year guaranteed minimum must be funded at the time of award, since that is the only amount to which the government is obligated. To comply with the ADA, then, additional funding must be put in place before additional orders are issued.

Preparation of a Bid

Generally, IFBs call for the bidder to fill out the government's solicitation form, unlike RFPs, which usually require submission of a filled-out bid form, plus a technical proposal. When filling out a bid, the bidder must follow the directions in the solicitation to the letter. While it is important in the case of a proposal or quote, it is critical in the case of an IFB. A bid must be in such a form that the government can award the contract with no further communication with or clarification from that bidder. Failure to complete the bid form properly, or taking exception to some requirement in the bid package, can render the bid "non-responsive," and a non-responsive bid cannot be corrected after bid opening; it must be rejected. Also bidders should never submit extraneous materials with a bid, such as overly-wordy cover letters, as they may serve to create an ambiguity. An ambiguous bid is a non-responsive one. A few years ago there was a situation where a bidder had properly completed the bid, but chose to include a cover letter with several statements that could have been read to suggest that the bidder was taking exception to a requirement of the solicitation. When the bidder protested the rejection of its bid to the Government Accountability Office (GAO), it argued that it had not taken any exceptions in its completed bid form and thus its bid should not have been rejected. However, the GAO ruled that any document submitted with a bid can be considered in determining the bid's responsiveness.

It is also important when submitting a bid that bidders acknowledge any amendments to the solicitation that may have been issued prior to the bid opening date. Failure to acknowledge a "material" amendment (an amendment that makes substantive changes to the solicitation's requirements) will render a bid non-responsive. While that is not true for amendments that are not "material," such as an amendment that simply changes the bid opening date, a bidder does not want to find itself in the position of arguing whether an amendment was "material." When submitting a bid, acknowledge all amendments by amendment number.

In many cases a solicitation will contemplate a multi-year contract. Generally these are set out as a base year and anywhere from one to four additional "option" years. In such situations, it should be noted that "option" refers to the government's right to have the contract continue for a second and a third year and so on, generally to a maximum of five years. The option is never the contractor's. In such situations, the solicitation will call for a bidder to price those option years at the time of submission of the bid. Obviously, if the solicitation is for award of a firm, fixed-priced contract, pricing work four or five years ahead of time is risky, since in the absence of some sort of adjustment clause the contractor will be stuck with the option prices in the offer. Should the solicitation call for bidders to price option years and a bidder does not, the bid will be rejected as non-responsive.

Most IFBs will specify an acceptance period, usually sixty or ninety days. During that acceptance period the bid is in the control of the government. A bidder cannot vary the government's acceptance period. Stating that prices are good for sixty days when the solicitation provides for a ninety-day acceptance period will render a bid non-responsive.

PREPARATION OF A PROPOSAL

In preparing a proposal in response to an RFP, an offeror must again follow the instructions, even though unlike IFB situations, a defective proposal may be corrected in the event the government elects to engage in negotiations with the offerors. Engaging in negotiations, however, based on what is stated in the RFP, is within the discretion of the contracting officer. An offeror does not want its status in the competition to depend on the government's discretion. Also, the same rules regarding mistakes or ambiguities in the bid package that apply to IFBs also apply to RFPs. If an offeror sees a mistake or ambiguity, it must report it to the contracting officer and try to get it corrected.

While RPFs, similar to IFBs, generally provide for a government acceptance period, in the case of an RFP an offer will not be rejected automatically for stating a shorter acceptance period. That is because the concept of responsiveness does not apply to solicitations in the case of negotiated procurements. Options are another matter. While a proposal that fails to price options cannot be rejected as non-responsive, the solicitation may advise offerors that a failure to price the options "may" result in rejection of a proposal as technically unacceptable. A few other pointers:

- Adhere to page limits and margin sizes. The government is free to disregard any part of a proposal or any information that is beyond the stated page limit or in the margins.

- Arrange the proposal in accordance with the instructions. If the solicitation says there should be one volume for price, one volume for past performance, and one volume for technical capability, then set up the proposal that way. Do not incorporate information from one part to another in an effort to avoid page limits.

- If the solicitation requests three past performance references, provide the three best. Do not provide six, for the government will disregard numbers four through six and if they happen to be better than the ones provided at numbers one through three, the proposal will be judged on numbers one through three only.

Another thing for an offeror to consider is protecting proprietary information. While bids in response to IFB are, by nature, publicly available, proposals in response to RFPs are not. If someone, say, a competitor, wants to see a proposal submitted in a certain competition, they can file a Freedom of Information Act (FOIA) request. Offerors will want to do all they can to protect their information from release. One way to do that is to put proprietary markings on the cover and on each page of the proposal. Something like "Contains Proprietary Information that is exempt from release under the Freedom of Information Act" should suffice. That will require the government agency to give the offeror a chance to review any information intended for release in response to an FOIA request. Marking information as "exempt" if it was not already exempt will not make it exempt, but it is a wise idea to err on the side of protecting everything. Also, if a solicitation requires offerors to provide information as part of their completed solicitation form, and the offeror does not want that information released (such as the name of a source for components) if someone files an FOIA request for the filled-out solicitation, the information should be submitted in a sealed envelope, with the protective legend on the outside of the envelope and on the page with the information itself. Then, in the appropriate place in the filled-out solicitation form, it should read, "See envelope attached."

Preparation of a Quotation

Requests for Quotes (RFQ) are the loosest of the procurement methods, and they are generally used in procurements below the Simplified Acquisition Threshold (SAT). That is because RFQs are considered to be informational. The government is requesting information regarding what price a company would charge for a specified product or service. It is request-ing that the company provide a quote in response. Should the government decide a certain quote is the one it wants, it does not award a contract. It sends the firm submitting the quote a contract form to sign and the firm can sign and accept the offer or decline to sign and reject the offer.

CONTRACTOR WARRANTIES

Most government solicitations will incorporate clauses providing that the contract will include various specific and general warranties of the products and services that the contractor will supply. Offerors would do well to make themselves familiar with them as part of their preparation for submitting a bid or proposal, for how such warranties operate can be very important in thinking about how to respond. Most of the standard warranty clauses allow the contracting officer to invoke the warranty unilaterally and direct the contractor to undertake the repair or replacement of the "defective" items. In extreme cases, the government may demand all of its money back. The government is not required to sue or otherwise prove that the items were defective. They will be presumed defective by virtue of the government's exercise of the warranty and the burden will be on the contractor to challenge the action by way of the contract's "Disputes" procedure (see Chapter 13).

SUBMISSION OF A BID OR PROPOSAL (TIMELINESS)

Perhaps the most critical factor when submitting a bid or proposal is the "timeliness" rule. The bid or proposal must arrive at the identified location at or before the stated time, i.e., "opening" time in the case of an IFB, "closing" time in the case of an RFP. A late bid or proposal may not be considered for award unless the lateness was the fault of the government. I offer a few pointers:

- If someone is hand-carrying the bid or proposal, leave ample time to arrive at the identified location. Most government offices and installations have stringent security rules and a bid or proposal that is late because the messenger was stuck in the security line is still late and cannot be considered.

- If the solicitation allows for submission of offers via e-mail or facsimile (and it must clearly state so), the entire proposal must arrive at the stated location before the scheduled time; if part of an electronically-submitted or facsimile-submitted proposal arrives after the stated time, the entire proposal is considered late. Be aware also, that when an offeror elects to submit the offer via facsimile, the offeror bears the risk of non-receipt, such as in the event of a machine malfunction.

- Bids or offers carried by FedEx and UPS are subject to the same rules as hand-carried bids and offers; their drivers must also go through security. However, a bid or proposal sent by USPS Priority Mail at least three (3) days before the due date will be considered timely regardless of when it arrives at the specified location, since the USPS is considered an arm of the government.

Bidders should be aware that no one has the authority to grant permission to submit a bid or offer after the stated date and time. A few years ago there was a situation where an offer had to arrive at an Air Force base in North Dakota. Due to snow, there was some doubt as to whether UPS or FedEx could get it there in time, so the offeror located a UPS store near the base and arranged for the offer to be sent there electronically; the store personnel stated they would get the offer delivered on time. The offeror, however, spoke with the contracting officer, who stated it would be sufficient if the offer arrived the following day, whereupon the offeror decided that the expense of using that local UPS store was unnecessary. The offer arrived the next day, but was subsequently rejected as late. The agency's position was that the contracting officer lacked the authority to change the due date for one offeror. Any change in the due date would have had to have been accomplished by way of an amendment to the solicitation so that all potential offerors would have had the benefit of the extra day. The GAO denied the offeror's protest against the rejection of its offer.

If offerors think the foregoing example was some sort of aberration, they should think again. In another recent situation, the solicitation simply stated that offers were due by "close of business" on the specified date. A potential offeror called the contracting officer and inquired as to what time was "close of business." The contracting officer responded that he went home at 5:00 p.m. each day. The offeror had its offer delivered shortly before 5:00 on the designated day, however, it was subsequently rejected as late. The FAR, it seems, deals with situations where a solicitation fails to set a specific time for receipt of offers: 4:30 p.m. local time (14.304(a) for IFBs and 15.208(a) for RFPs). Once again, the contracting officer lacked the authority to set a different time for one offeror, and once again the GAO denied the offeror's protest against the rejection of its "late" offer.

Offerors can bear in mind that the timeliness rules do not apply to RFQs. Quotations submitted in response to RFQs are considered "informational" in that the government does not "award" a contract in an RFQ competition. Unless the RFQ has a specific clause stating that late submissions will not be considered, the government is free to consider a quotation no matter when it is received so long as there is no prejudice to other offerors.

Withdrawal of a Bid, Offer, or Quotation

What happens if an offeror decides after submission of a bid, offer, or quotation that it no longer wants the contract? Perhaps it has been awarded another contract and no longer has the capacity to perform. How can a bid, offer, or quote be withdrawn? The answer depends on the type of procurement.

In the case of publicly-opened bids, the bid must be withdrawn prior to the opening. A bidder that wants to withdraw its bid should send a letter, timed to arrive before the time for opening the bids, directing the contracting officer to disregard the bid. The letter or facsimile (if permitted) must be submitted just as if it were itself a bid: it must arrive before the time scheduled for opening of the bids. Once bids are opened a bidder can no longer withdraw the bid, unless it can prove a mistake.

In the case of a negotiated procurement, as noted earlier, there are no restrictions on withdrawal of an offer. An offeror can withdraw its offer at any time prior to the government awarding it the contract; no reason is required. The offeror need only send in a letter informing the government that the offer is withdrawn.

For a quotation there is no need to withdraw. Remember, quotations are informational only. The government must make an offer of an order, and the recipient of the offer can simply decline the order.

Mistakes in Bids—Clerical, Mathematical, Judgmental

A bidder submits its bid or offer and suddenly realizes there was a mistake in it. What can be done? The answer depends on the type of mistake (mathematical, clerical, or judgmental), when it is discovered, and to some degree what type of competition was involved (publicly-opened bids or contracting by negotiation, for example).

If the procurement is being conducted by publicly-opened bids and the bidder realizes there is a mistake prior to the opening of bids, the bidder should send in a timely corrected bid with instructions to the contracting officer to disregard the prior one. If the bids have been opened, matters become more complicated. If the mistaken bid is the lowest one, but there is a mathematical or clerical mistake that will cost the bidder a significant loss if it is forced to perform, relief is generally available. In the case of a mathematical mistake (such as a mistake in addition or multiplication) or a clerical mistake (transposing numbers, for example), the mistake will likely be fairly easy to recognize. Assuming the correct bid can be determined from the face of the filled-out solicitation, the bidder will be allowed to correct the mistake. The rules for publicly-opened bids do not allow the government to take advantage of a bidder's mistake. Indeed, if a bid is strikingly lower than all of the others, so that the government should suspect that there is a mistake, the contracting officer is required under FAR 14.407-1 to point out to the bidder that the low bid may indicate a mistake and request that the bidder verify its price. In fact, if the contracting officer fails to ask a bidder to verify its pricing when a bidding mistake should have been suspected, and instead simply awards the contract, the bidder will likely be able to avoid performing. In fact, a contractor may even be able to have its price increased to the correct figure (called "reformation"), if the government insists that the contract be performed at the mistaken price.

What about a mistake in judgment? Suppose a bid was based on assumptions of efficiency that were impossibly optimistic? Generally there is no relief in such a case. The only hope would be that the bid was so low that the government should have suspected the mistake, bringing FAR 14.407-1 into play. If the government requests verification of the bid, the bidder should be allowed to withdraw the bid, since forcing a bidder who did not verify its bid to perform will likely result in reformation later at a higher cost to the government.

What happens in a situation where a bid is not low because of a mathematical or clerical mistake? Can an erroneous bid be corrected so that it is now the lowest bid? Once again the question revolves around whether the correct bid can be determined from the face of the bid itself, for example an error in the total price due to an error in adding the unit pricing. In such a case, the bid will be corrected. If, on the other hand, the mistake can only be determined by looking at some other documents, such as original notes to show that the bidder wrote the wrong number on the bid, that bidder will likely not be permitted to change its bid and dislodge a lower bidder. The integrity of the system is paramount. To allow someone to lower its bid price after bid opening by claiming that the price was written down incorrectly would encourage bidders to submit high prices to see if they can win the contract at one price, and then come in with a lower price after seeing the other bids by claiming the submitted price was a mistake.

In the case of a competition using negotiated procedures, if an offeror realizes the mistake before the closing date, it can send in a corrected offer. If the mistake is discovered after the closing date for offers but before the award, as discussed above, the offeror can withdraw its offer. If the government elects not to conduct discussions, there will be no opportunity for an offeror to correct its mistaken offer. There is also no specific rule in the case of procurements conducted by negotiation requiring contracting officers to seek verification of an offer where a mistake is or should be suspected, such as is the case with FAR 14.407-1 for publicly-opened bids. The courts have, however, suggested that the right of the government to conduct clarifications with a single offeror provides the opportunity for correction of mistakes and a contracting officer should seek a clarification when a mistake is suspected.

What if the mistake is not obvious but the offeror would rather not withdraw its offer? If the government engages in discussions the offeror will have an opportunity when discussions are completed to submit a revised offer, meaning an opportunity to correct the mistake. If, however, the government does not conduct discussions, the offeror will not have an opportunity to submit a corrected offer.

CONCLUSION

If you take nothing else from this chapter, take a few rules to heart. Take the time necessary to complete the solicitation form properly; you may not have the opportunity to correct mistakes. If the solicitation is a request for proposals, make sure to address all of the evaluation factors and do so within the page limits if page limits are specified. Finally, and perhaps most importantly, leave sufficient time to ensure that your proposal arrives at the agency by the due date and time. A wonderfully written and competitively priced proposal is worthless if it arrives five minutes late.

Chapter 9

CONTRACT AWARDS AND COMPETITION CONTROVERSIES

When you consider the size of the FAR, together with the other regulations that apply to government procurements, and you also consider the amount of dollars that are involved in many government competitions, it should come as no great wonder that government solicitations and contract awards have generated and will continue to generate a considerable amount of litigation. These cases are referred to as "protests." In this chapter I will discuss some of the issues that give rise to protests, as well as the procedures for initiating and pursuing protests.

SOLICITATION REQUIREMENTS: RESPONSIVENESS VERSUS RESPONSIBILITY

The government can only award contracts to bidders or offerors who are both "responsive" and "responsible." The term "responsive" is generally applicable to contracts awarded through publicly opened bids. It refers to a bidder's unconditional "response" to the solicitation and will be discussed in more detail below. The term "responsible" is applicable to all procurements and refers to the ability of a bidder or offeror to perform the contract to be awarded, generally referred to as "capacity and credit," e.g., sufficient financing, numbers of personnel, or machinery (if applicable).

Given the importance, the distinction between "responsiveness" and "responsibility" has spawned considerable protest litigation. Much of it occurs in solicitations that require a specific license from a state or local municipality in order to perform the contract. In general, the requirement for a license, according to the GAO, is a matter of "responsibility," meaning it relates to the contractor's ability to perform the contract. As such, a requirement for license can be satisfied at or before the time of the award. The purpose of such a requirement being considered one of responsibility makes sense, as it would seem pointless to have anyone who would like to submit a bid go through the expense of procuring some sort of local license which, in the case of everyone but the awardee, may well never be used. The fact that a solicitation may refer to the need for such a license as a requirement for "responsiveness" makes no difference. What a solicitation calls a requirement cannot convert it from one of "responsibility" to one of "responsiveness."

That having been said, on occasion a matter that is one of responsibility can rise to a level approaching that of responsiveness, meaning a failure to include the required information will result in rejection of a proposal. The term used is "definitive responsibility criteria," and it refers to a situation where a solicitation requires a contractor to submit some specific evidence that it meets a requirement as part of its proposal. A good example would be a contract for a residential reentry center (in other words, a group halfway house for inmates to be integrated back into society). A requirement that a proposal include proof of zoning approval would be such a definitive responsibility criteria and failure to include such proof will likely result in rejection of the proposal. Likewise, in some service contracts the government requires employees with specific education or training. In that event, the solicitation will require submission of resumes as part of the technical proposal, and a failure to include the resumes will result in the rejection of the offer as technically unacceptable.

Bidders should also keep in mind that when the contract to be awarded is the firm, fixed-price type, there is no rule that bars the government from accepting a ridiculously low or even below-cost bid or offer. If a bidder is willing to perform at no profit or even absorb a loss to get that contract, the government will certainly allow it.

PRE-AWARD SURVEYS

A pre-award survey is a review to a potential awardee's ability to perform the contract to be awarded. It is used to determine the prospective contractor's "responsibility."

Pre-award surveys are most often used where the contract is to be awarded through publicly-opened bids, because in that case, unlike competitions using negotiated procedures, there are no technical proposals and no exchanges between the offeror and the government to resolve questions regarding the offeror's ability to perform the contract. In a pre-award survey, government technical and financial specialists will review every aspect of the potential awardee's operation, such as the size of its facility, the availability of any required machinery, the number and training of employees, and the firm's financial capability. A positive pre-award survey report does not guarantee award of the contract, but a negative one will almost certainly mean that the potential awardee will not receive it, so it would behoove a firm to cooperate fully with the survey team. Hence the adequacy of a pre-award survey is another area that can spawn a protest.

PROTESTS TO THE AGENCY

Offerors who perceive a problem with a solicitation or feel they have been treated wrongly in a competition are encouraged to take their complaint in the first instance to the contracting agency itself. Most agencies have established procedures for handling such protests, and they are specifically covered in FAR Subpart 33.1. Taking a protest to the agency first can help maintain a good relationship with the agency, since the offeror is giving them the first opportunity to correct what it perceives as an impropriety or injustice. Going the agency protest route does not foreclose an offeror from going to the GAO, should it be dissatisfied with the agency's decision on a protest. The time to protest to GAO does not begin to run until there is a decision on an agency protest. In terms of time for filing an agency protest, the same rules that apply to GAO protests apply to agency protests. Offerors should check the individual solicitation, as it will likely specify the specific person to whom an agency protest should be submitted.

PROTESTS TO THE GOVERNMENT ACCOUNTABILITY OFFICE (GAO)

Most disputes arising out of competitions are pursued at the Government Accountability Office (GAO). Under the Competition in Contracting Act (CICA), the GAO has authority to hear and resolve most disputes involving solicitations and award decisions by agencies of the Executive Branch (but not the legislative or judicial branches). The big advantage in taking a protest to the GAO is cost: there is (currently) no filing fee and a protester does not have to have a lawyer. I should note, though, that in most cases involving competitions conducted using negotiation, consideration of a protest involves reviewing agency evaluations and source selection documents. Such documents cannot be disclosed to individual competitors, so when a protester handles the protest without an outside attorney, there will be no access to those materials. If the protester uses an outside attorney in the protest, the attorney can see the evaluations and source selection documents under the terms of the GAO's standard protective order (by which the attorney certifies he or she will not disclose the materials to the client).

It is important to bear in mind that in order to maintain a protest to the GAO, there must be "standing." That means a protester must have some economic interest it is entitled to protect. For example, a firm cannot protest a contract award if it was not a bidder or offeror. That means a firm that is in line to receive a subcontract if the contract were to be awarded to a bidder or offeror has no right to bring the protest. Nor could a firm protest an award arising from a HUBZone set-aside competition if it is not itself a certified HUBZone contractor. Also, the GAO will not sustain a protest without a showing of "prejudice." What that means is it is not sufficient for a protester to show that there were errors committed by the government in a competition. A protester must be able to show that, but for the errors, it would have had a substantial chance of receiving the contract award—not a certainty, but a substantial chance. For example, proving that a technical proposal should have been rated "good" rather than "acceptable" will not be sufficient for GAO to sustain a protest when the awardee's proposal was rated "very good" and the awardee offered a lower price than the protester did.

As I am mentioning subcontractors and their inability to protest the award of a prime contract, there is no forum in which a proposed subcontractor can protest the failure by a prime contractor who received the award to issue it a subcontract. The only exception to this rule is a situation where, even though technically the government would not be a party to the subcontract, it controlled the process of the prime contractor's selection of subcontractors. The inability of a would-be subcontractor to protest the failure of the prime contractor to issue the subcontract is the rule even where there was a teaming agreement in place designating the would-be subcontractor as part of the performance team. It is why, as I stressed in Chapter 5, Teaming Agreements, it is critical to nail down every aspect of future contract performance. It still will not give the subcontractor a vehicle to bring a protest, but it may allow for a court action seeking damages for breach of contract.

Contractors considering pursuing a protest will often ask, "If I file a protest, won't the agency personnel hold it against me?" Certainly challenging the actions of someone who, it is hoped, will become a long-term customer is not an ideal situation. Most contracting officers understand, however, that protests are a part of the system and that they are not a personal attack.

Indeed, making a protest a personal attack is likely a pointless exercise. The GAO (as well as the Court of Federal Claims) applies a legal presumption that government officials carry out their duties in good faith. A protester who alleges that contracting officials were biased against it must produce "direct evidence" proving that bias. "Direct evidence" means something more than the normal standard in a civil case, i.e., a preponderance of the evidence, and approaching that of a criminal case, i.e., beyond a reasonable doubt. The mere fact that decisions were made that the protester challenges does not prove bias, according to the GAO, even if the decisions were erroneous. Given how difficult it is to win a protest by claiming bias on the part of agency officials, offerors should go down that path only with hard evidence in hand. I have often told clients who are thinking of pursuing a protest on the basis that agency evaluators were prejudiced against them that if they hope to win such a protest, they had better have a sworn affidavit from someone in the room who overhead the evaluator promising to "get" that contractor.

So long as a firm does not get a reputation as one that protests everything or engages in unsupported personal attacks on agency officials, an occasional protest will not be viewed negatively. In fact, there are numerous examples of situations where it was only by one of the unsuccessful offerors filing a protest that an improper award was discovered. For example, several years ago, the Army initiated a negotiated "Best Value" procurement to provide meats to military installations in the Northeast. The solicitation required offerors to propose pricing based on a requirement that they be available to deliver product seven days a week, as required by the various installations. One offeror took exception to that requirement and proposed that it would only deliver to each installation in accordance with a set weekly schedule and the installations had to place orders to conform to that schedule. Not surprisingly, that offeror had the lowest price. The Army contracting officer requested that the offeror withdraw the exception, but the offeror refused. That offeror was then awarded the contract. A losing offeror filed what might be called a "generic" protest with GAO, challenging the Army's best value determination. Remember, because this was a negotiated procurement, the awardee's offer with its exception to the solicitation delivery requirements was not disclosed to other offerors. However, in the course of the protest, the attorneys for the protester gained access to the awardee's offer and discovered the exception it had taken.

They immediately added that exception as an additional protest ground. The GAO sustained the protest, ruling that an award to an offeror who takes exception to a material requirement of a solicitation is improper. If the Army could live with the exception the awardee took, GAO stated, then all offerors should have been given the opportunity to offer based on that exception. In the end, it was only by filing a protest that the fact that the awardee had taken exception to the solicitation's delivery requirement was discovered.

APPEALS OF THE DESIGNATION OF THE NAICS CODE IN A SMALL BUSINESS SET-ASIDE

Given the importance of the designation of the appropriate NAICS code by the contracting officer in a small business set-aside competition (see Chapter 4, Socioeconomic Programs), SBA regulations allow for a potential offeror who would be excluded from the competition under the designated NAICS code, but who would be eligible under a different code, to appeal the designation. Appeals are to be submitted to the SBA Office of Hearings and Appeals (OHA), and must be filed with the OHA within ten (10) days of the issuance of the solicitation in order to be timely. The OHA has no discretion to waive the filing deadline.

PROTESTS AGAINST THE TERMS OF A SOLICITATION

If a potential bidder believes a solicitation contains an improper provision or is somehow ambiguous, it has the right to submit a protest to the GAO. However, there are strict time limits for such protests, and failure to abide by them can get a protest dismissed.

Under GAO regulations, any protest against the terms of a solicitation must be filed before the due date for bids or offers. A bidder cannot sit back and wait to see if it wins the award and then protest the rules of the competition if it does not. The only exception to this rule is a situation involving a latent ambiguity. If after award to the competitor a bidder realizes that the solicitation contained an ambiguity that was not readily apparent and which worked to its disadvantage in the competition, it can protest after the award. However, in such a case the bidder must file its protest within ten days of the date it first realized there was an ambiguity (or when it should have first realized it). If the problem or ambiguity arises through an agency's amendment of a solicitation, then a protest must be submitted to GAO before the next due date for revised offers. If the amendment does not allow for revised offers, then the normal ten-day rule applicable to "negotiated" procurements governs.

PROTESTS AGAINST BUNDLING

A frequent issue in GAO pre-award protests is "bundling." That term refers to combining different types of requirements in a way that forecloses participation by small businesses. For example, a solicitation may call for the contractor to supply manufactured products and also provide warehousing for those products until the government requires delivery. Generally, if the products and services have been procured separately in the past, the GAO will sustain a protest against the new "bundled" solicitation. If, however, the requirements have been bundled in the past, or the requirement is considered "new," so as not to qualify as having been procured in the past, the GAO will not sustain a protest.

PROTESTS AGAINST AGENCY ADVERSE ACTION

If a bid is rejected or a proposal excluded from the competitive range before an award is made, the bidder or offeror is required to protest at that point. The offeror cannot sit back and then, when it sees that the contract went to someone whose price was higher than its own, file a protest. GAO's protest rules require that any such protest must be filed within ten days of the date the offeror learns of "adverse action" by the agency. The days may be extended by submitting a timely (i.e., within three days) request for a debriefing, and a debriefing is required (generally applicable to "negotiated" procurements). In such a case, the time to protest begins to run on the first date the agency offers for the debriefing.

The entitlement to a debriefing has caused many protesters considerable trouble. When a proposal is excluded from a competition conducted using negotiated procedures, as noted above, the offeror has three days to request a debriefing. Usually agency officials will explain that the debriefing can be then (a pre-award debriefing) or after the award is made to another offeror (a post-award debriefing). They will say that they will be able to provide much more information in a post-award debriefing, most notably information involving the awardee. By opting for the post-award debriefing, however, the offeror will lose its right to protest the exclusion of its offer from the competition, because the ten-day clock to protest started when the proposal was excluded. Awaiting the award decision and post-award debriefing to protest the exclusion of a proposal means the protest will be dismissed as untimely. Nor could a protest against the award to the winning offeror be filed after the award, since at that point the excluded firm was no longer an offeror in the competition and thus not eligible for the award. The GAO will not consider a protest by an offeror who would not be eligible to receive the award if the protest were to be sustained.

By filing a timely pre-award protest, whether against the terms of a solicitation or against the rejection of a proposal, the agency withholds the contract award until the protest is resolved, in accordance with the requirements of CICA.

Post-Award Protests to the GAO

An offeror who believes a contract was improperly awarded and should have gone to it instead can file a post-award protest with the GAO. The timeliness rules allow ten days to file such a protest. As with pre-award protests, though, by making a timely (within three days of notification of the name of the awardee) request for a post-award debriefing, the ten days does not begin to run until the first date offered by the agency for the debriefing. There is one caveat to be aware of: under CICA, when the agency receives notice of the filing of a protest from GAO within five days of the date of award (or five days after the first date offered for the post-award debriefing, whichever is later), the agency must suspend all contract performance until resolution of the protest. While the GAO generally notifies the agency within minutes of receipt of a protest, protests should be submitted in sufficient time to allow for the GAO's turn-around time. Protesters should always keep in mind that the GAO strictly construes its timeliness regulations. Even in a situation where the awardee of a contract had submitted a non-responsive bid, the GAO will dismiss an untimely protest and allow the award to the non-responsive bidder stand.

It is post-award protests where the concepts of "standing" and "prejudice" are in many cases the determining factor in GAO denying or dismissing a protest. In a competition conducted by sealed bidding, if a protester is not the second low bidder, it does not have "standing" to protest the award to the low bidder, because it would not be in line for the award even if it won the protest. To have "standing" in such a case, a protester would have to protest all the bidders in front of it. In a negotiated "Best Value" type procurement, on the other hand, any offeror who was in the competitive range when the final award decision was made would have "standing" to challenge the evaluations by asserting that its offer was improperly evaluated or that the source selection decision (i.e., the cost-technical trade-off) was not in accordance with the terms of the solicitation or the FAR. Of course a protester's proposal would have had to have been at least somewhere in the neighborhood of the awardee, or the GAO might well decide that its chances of ultimately winning the award were too remote to establish "prejudice" and dismiss the protest for lack of standing.

What happens if the GAO agrees that an unsuccessful offeror has standing to pursue a protest? The GAO will not substitute its judgment for that of agency contracting officials. Rather, the GAO reviews all the procurement-related documents (e.g., the proposals, the evaluations, and the source selection decision) to determine if the agency's evaluations and source selection decision complied with the mandates of the FAR and the terms of that particular solicitation. Only where there is a clear violation of regulations or a failure to comply with the evaluation methodology outlined in the solicitation will a protest be sustained.

What rights does the offeror that received the award have when another offeror protests? GAO regulations allow an awardee to intervene in the protest to protect its award. An awardee is considered an "interested party" in the protest. The same rules regarding access to source selection materials apply to an interested party as apply to the protester. Access to such materials is restricted to outside attorneys admitted to the GAO protective order. Unfortunately, while the law allows a successful protester to recover the cost of pursuing its protest, there is no corresponding rule that would allow an interested party that participates in a successful defense against a protest to recoup its legal expense.

Remedies Available in a GAO Protest

First, the GAO does not have the authority to direct a contracting agency to do anything. It makes recommendations, which agencies will almost always (although not always) follow. One attractive aspect of taking a protest to the GAO, though, is that if the protest is successful and is sustained, the GAO will award the protester the cost of pursuing the protest, with the cost to be paid by the contracting agency. In fact, even in a case where the agency elects not to contest the protest and opts instead to take "corrective action," the GAO may "recommend" that the agency reimburse protest costs if it determines that the agency delayed taking the corrective action in the face of a protest that was "clearly meritorious."

Protests to the Court of Federal Claims (CFC)

Rather than bringing a protest to the GAO, an unsuccessful offeror can file it with the Court of Federal Claims (CFC). The advantage is that the CFC gets far fewer protests than the GAO, so more attention can be given to each, and protests are heard by federal judges rather than GAO staff attorneys. The disadvantages are that a protester must have an attorney file a protest and there is a filing fee, as with any other lawsuit. I generally recommend the CFC for protests involving procurements of significant dollar value. CFC judges review agency action in accordance with the requirements of the Administrative Procedure Act (APA). Under the APA, it is not sufficient for the judge to disagree with the decisions of an agency. The decision must be "arbitrary and capricious" or "lacking a rational basis." As with the GAO, the protester must establish standing and prejudice.

The CFC does not have formal timeliness rules (meaning no ten-day or five-day deadlines). The only rule is that a protester act promptly; delay can be fatal to a protest, since judges are reluctant to overly delay the government from proceeding with performance of a contract. As with the GAO, a protest against the terms of a solicitation must be filed before the due date for bids or offers. Also, unlike CICA's stop-work requirements for GAO protests, there is no automatic stop-work order in a CFC protest. If the government does not agree to suspend performance voluntarily, then it is up to the judge to decide whether to issue a temporary injunction.

In some cases, protesters who are dissatisfied with a decision by GAO will then file the protest in the CFC. While CFC judges give deference to decisions by the GAO, they are not binding on the CFC. In fact, I have seen a number of cases where CFC judges have found a GAO decision to be irrational and directed the government not to follow it. Indeed this seems to have been happening with greater frequency in recent years.

Remedies Available in the CFC

While GAO decisions are recommendations, CFC decisions are generally in the form of injunctions that the government must follow. However, as with any other legal action, the issuance of an injunction is generally within the discretion of the particular judge. In deciding whether to enjoin the government from proceeding on a contract where agency action has been found to have been improper, the CFC judges are required to weigh the harm to the protester if an injunction is not issued versus the harm to the government if one is issued, say the delay on a much-needed road project, for example. In such a case the judge may rule in favor of the protester, but decline to issue an injunction. The protester is awarded its bid preparation costs, which in most cases involving small businesses are fairly insubstantial. Under no circumstances can a protester be awarded its lost profit (i.e., the profit it would have earned had it received the contract award it should have received).

With respect to recouping protest costs, unlike the GAO there is no automatic rule that a winning protester gets reimbursed the cost of pursuing the protest. The CFC awards legal fees in accordance with the requirements of the Equal Access to Justice Act (EAJA). See Chapter 13, Disputes.

PROTESTS AGAINST AWARDS OF TASK OR DELIVERY ORDERS UNDER MULTIPLE AWARD CONTRACTS

Congress has opted to place limits on offerors' rights to protest task or delivery order awards competed under multiple award task order contracts (MATOCs). By law, the CFC has no jurisdiction to hear a protest against any award of a task or delivery order under a MATOC. As for the GAO, its jurisdiction to consider such protests is limited to task and delivery orders valued at over $10 million. The only right granted to the competing contractors in a task order competition valued at under $10 million is a complaint to the agency ombudsman.

Status Protests

In any sort of set-aside procurement, an unsuccessful offeror can challenge the status of the awardee. For example, if a competitor believes the awardee in a small business set-aside is not in fact small, it can initiate a "size protest." Even though it is the Small Business Administration (SBA) that decides size protests, a protester must initiate a protest by submitting its challenge to the contracting officer who awarded the contract. The contracting officer must then forward the protest to SBA for resolution. The only requirements are (1) that the protest must be submitted within five days of the date that the name of the awardee is published, and (2) that the protest be "specific." Concerning the five days, governing regulations require that contracting officers provide the unsuccessful offerors in a small business set-aside competition notice of the proposed awardee at least three (3) days prior to award, so as to allow sufficient time to submit a protest. If the contracting officer fails to provide the advance notice, then the five-day clock begins to run when notice of the actual award is circulated. With regard to the second requirement, by "specific" it means that it is not sufficient to say simply, "I do not believe the awardee is small." That will get the protest summarily dismissed by SBA. To constitute a valid size protest, the submission must offer some evidence in support of the accusation, such as a D&B report, newspaper articles, or information gleaned from Internet research, and it must be included with the protest. There will be no second chance later.

The same procedures apply to protests involving HUBZone status or WOSB/EDWOSB status as apply to size protests. These are decided by SBA, but once again, the protest must be submitted to the contracting officer. There are special requirements for VOSB and SDVOSB status challenges. In the case of a VA procurement, it is the VA that decides the protest. If the procurement is conducted by any agency other than the VA, however, the protest is decided by the SBA. Interestingly, while a protest to the VA alleging that an awardee is not on the VA's register of certified VOSB or SDVOSB contractors is sufficient to maintain a protest, a protest on that basis submitted to SBA in a non-VA procurement will be dismissed as insufficiently specific. Since offerors on non-VA procurements can self-certify their VOSB or SDVOSB status, merely alleging that the awardee is not on the VA's list is not enough to constitute a valid protest; specific information about the awardee is required.

Special rules govern status protests involving 8(a) set-aside procurements. A competitor cannot protest an awardee's qualifications as a certified 8(a) contractor, since the awardee's eligibility was established by SBA when it certified the firm for admission to the 8(a) Program in the first instance. A competitor can, however, protest that an 8(a) awardee is no longer a small business. If an 8(a) program participant becomes large, it is automatically ousted from the program and, of course, would be ineligible for an 8(a) set-aside award. An 8(a) awardee's size can be challenged by following the same procedures and requirements as for any other size protest.

CONCLUSION

Unfortunately, in the world of government contracting, winning the competition may be just the beginning of your struggle. You may have to fight to hold onto what you have won, because, unlike the commercial world, unsuccessful bidders on government contracts have the right to "protest" virtually any award decision. Of course, if you are an unsuccessful bidder some time, that right may come in handy. However, bear in mind that not every potential fight is worth fighting. Hopefully I have given you enough of a primer so that you can decide when it is worthwhile to protest and when to bide your time until another day.

Chapter 10

CONTRACT ADMINISTRATION

I n Chapter 1, Getting Started, I discussed the authority of government employees, mostly in reference to contracting, but it bears repeating in the area of contract administration. In performing on a government contract, a contractor will deal with any number of government officials and employees. There may be multiple contracting officers, for example, as contracts are issued by a Procuring Contracting Officer (PCO) and may be administered by an Administrative Contracting Officer (ACO). There may be on-site government inspectors, possibly referred to as Quality Assurance Representatives (QAR) for manufacturing contracts or Contracting Officer's Representatives (COR) for service contracts. A contractor may deal with architects or engineers on a construction project. It is the contractor's responsibility to know the limits of a government employee's authority before following any of their instructions, for actions beyond the authority of a government employee cannot bind the government. It does not matter that the employee or official believes he or she has the necessary authority. The contractor is responsible for verifying their authority. There is one simple rule to follow: no one but a contracting officer (generally only the PCO) can change the terms of a contract. A QAR or COR may want things done a certain way, despite what the contract says. A contractor following instructions from a QAR or COR without getting verification from the PCO is asking for trouble, because aside from costing the contractor money, it can result in its performance being judged unacceptable.

Perhaps the best (or worst) illustration of this principle was a case several years ago involving instructions (both written and oral) given to a contractor at a post-award conference (a sort of contract kick-off meeting, establishing the guidelines for contract performance and administration). The contractor was instructed at the conference to follow the directives provided by the COR. The contractor did as instructed, following directions that involved extra work and extra costs. When it sought payment for the extra costs, its request was denied. It pursued its claim under the Contract Disputes Act, but was ultimately unsuccessful. It seems the instructions the contractor had been given at the post-award conference were incorrect. Under the contract, the COR did not have the authority to direct the contractor to perform extra work, meaning, as far as the government was concerned, the work had not been ordered by the government. What about the instructions to follow the COR's directives that the contractor was given by the government personnel at the post-award conference? It seems that the contracting officer was not in attendance at the post-award conference. Thus, the instructions which varied from the contract's terms were not given to the contractor by anyone who had the authority to change the contract's terms. Hence the contractor should not have followed those instructions without getting confirmation from the contracting officer. Had the contracting officer been in attendance and at least heard the instructions when they were given, the outcome would have been different, but the contracting officer had not been present.

CHANGES

In a principle that is almost totally unique to government contracts, most such contracts contain a "Changes" clause. The standard changes clause gives the contracting officer (the PCO) the right to make almost any change in the contract that the government deems necessary or beneficial. The authority to make such changes is unilateral; the contractor's agreement is not required. The only limitation on that authority is that the change must be within the scope of the contract. A contract for books cannot be changed to a contract for automobiles. That is referred to as a "Cardinal Change," meaning a change of such magnitude that it essentially represents a new contract which, under the Competition in Contracting Act, must be awarded through competition.

Formal changes to a contract are accomplished by a modification, signed by an authorized contracting officer. Modifications can be "unilateral" (meaning signed by the contracting officer alone, under authority of the "Changes" clause) or "bilateral" (meaning signed by both parties), and there is a significant difference. When a change is unilaterally imposed on a contractor and it adds to the effort, the contractor is entitled to additional compensation for the additional work. On the other hand, contracting officers will occasionally request that a contractor sign the modification, indicating agreement to the change. Signing such a modification without reserving the right to seek additional compensation for the change is a huge mistake. It will allow the government to argue later that the contractor agreed to the change at no extra cost. That is why contracting officers will often request the contractor's signature on a modification that the government wants. While it may be possible to avoid the effects of signing such a modification later (on the grounds that there was no "consideration" flowing to the contractor in the agreement), no one needs the expense and risk of litigation.

Under the terms of the "Changes" clause, assuming there has been a directive from the contracting officer, a contractor must perform in accordance with the changed work while the parties settle any issues arising from the directive. Refusal can result in a termination for default (see below), even if the position that the change was improper is later upheld by a court or agency board of contract appeals. The contractor's remedy in the event of a change that it believes was improper is by way of the contract's "Disputes" provisions.

COMPENSATION FOR CHANGES (EQUITABLE ADJUSTMENTS)

When its contract has been changed, a contractor is entitled to a change in the contract's price (called an "Equitable

Adjustment"). The contractor gets that adjustment by submitting a proposal, referred to as a Request for Equitable Adjustment (REA), to cover the cost increase (or decrease) caused by the changed work. Once the proposal is audited, the contractor and the contracting officer will attempt to negotiate the price adjustment, which may be up or down, depending on whether the changes added or deleted work. If the parties are unable to reach an agreement on the adjustment, the contracting officer has the right to adjust the contract price unilaterally. If a contractor is dissatisfied with the contracting officer's unilateral decision, it may invoke its rights under the "Disputes" clause by submitting a "claim." See Chapter 13, Disputes.

It is imperative that contractors understand and abide by the time limits for asserting the right to an adjustment in the event the government makes changes in the contract under the "Changes" clause. The standard clause requires the contractor, if it believes there is a cost impact resulting from a government-mandated change, to assert its right to an adjustment within thirty days from the date of the change. That does not mean a contractor has to know precisely what the cost impact will be. It is sufficient that it assert its right to an adjustment and provide whatever information is available at that point documenting the right to a price adjustment.

As discussed, the starting point for negotiating the price adjustment for changed work is the submission of an REA. There is no special format for an REA. A letter can suffice so long as it sets out the facts in a logical manner and explains the methodology used to determine the amount of the request. The one caveat is a requirement for DOD contracts.

Per DFAR 252.243-7002, any REA submitted under a DOD contract that exceeds the Simplified Acquisition Threshold must include the following certification language:

> I certify that the request is made in good faith, and that the supporting data are accurate and complete to the best of my knowledge and belief.

The certification should be signed by an official with authority to bind the contractor, complete with his or her title. The DFAR provision states that this certification requires disclosure of all relevant facts, including certified cost or pricing data if required under FAR 15.403-4 or data other than certified cost or pricing data, in accordance with FAR 15.403-3, including data to support any estimated costs.

Truth in Negotiations Act

The conduct of any negotiations for an "Equitable Adjustment" in the contract's price is subject to very stringent rules. Under the Truth in Negotiations Act (TINA) a contractor is required to disclose all information in its possession that could affect the government's position in the negotiations. In other words, when "sitting down at the table," figuratively speaking, a contractor is required to show the government's negotiators all of its cards up front. At the conclusion of the negotiations, the contractor will be required to sign a "Certificate of Current Cost or Price Data," certifying that it has disclosed to the government all current information in its possession or of which it is aware. Remember that the government has a right to audit a contractor's books following contract completion, and should the auditors discover that there was information the contractor failed to disclose (such as actually projecting a higher efficiency than what was given to the government negotiators), the contractor can be subject to civil or criminal "defective pricing" penalties.

To give an example of how strict the TINA requirements are, a reported decision some years ago involved a government defective pricing claim against a major weapons contractor. It seems that the contractor and the government had negotiated a price adjustment for government-directed changes. One part of the adjustment involved a purchased component. At the conclusion of the negotiations the contractor provided the government with the TINA "Certificate of Current Cost or Price Data." However, at the time the contractor signed the certificate, it had in its possession unopened bids from several sources to supply the purchased component. The bids had not been opened as of the date of the TINA certificate, because the final date for receipt of such bids had not arrived as yet. It did not matter that the bids for the purchased component had not been opened. Their mere existence was a fact that had to be disclosed in the negotiations with the government, thereby rendering the contractor's TINA certificate false.

One factor to bear in mind when attempting to negotiate an Equitable Adjustment is the purpose of an Equitable Adjustment; it is not to make a contractor "well." If contract performance is running at a 15 percent loss and the government adds additional work, the price adjustment for that additional work will have the same 15 percent loss built into it. A contractor cannot be made better off by a change than it was before. By the same token, if a contract is running at a 15 percent profit and the government adds additional work, the price adjustment for that additional work should include the same 15 percent profit. A contractor cannot be made worse off by a change than it was before.

As an aside, contractors should be aware that the FAR cost principles provide that any legal and accounting expense incurred in preparing and negotiating an REA are considered allowable costs. They can be included in the REA and are fully reimbursable up to the point where the contractor concludes there cannot be a settlement and that it will pursue its disputes rights. Legal expense related to preparing and negotiating an REA are allowable; those related to preparing and pursuing a claim are not.

Constructive Changes

In addition to formal contractual changes, accomplished by way of a contract modification, there are occasionally what are called "constructive" changes. From time to time the government contracting officer may direct the contractor to carry out the work in a manner that the contractor believes amounts to a change in the contract, even though the contracting officer does not issue a formal modification. Indeed, in some situations the contracting officer may deny that the directive was even a change. The requirements for a constructive change are: (1) the government compelled the contractor to perform work not required by the contract;

(2) the government official directing the contractor to do the work had the contracting authority to do so; (3) the contractor's duties were enlarged due to the directive; and (4) the contractor was not a "volunteer," but only did the extra work as a result of the directive.

Regardless of whether a contractor believes the work it is being directed to do was required under the contract, it is still required to follow the contracting officer's directives. If a contractor truly believes the directives amount to a change to the contract, then it must promptly advise the contracting officer of its position and assert its right to a price adjustment. Unlike a formal change order, which triggers the running of the thirty-day period for asserting the right to an adjustment, there is no set time limit for notice in the case of "constructive" changes. The requirement that a contractor assert its right to an adjustment promptly is designed to allow the government the opportunity to reevaluate its position and, perhaps, resolve the disagreement before the contractor incurs significant costs following the directive.

EXCUSABLE DELAYS; STOP WORK ORDERS

There are two types of delays in reference to performing on a government contract: excusable and inexcusable. Excusable delays are those that occur through no fault of the contractor. Examples include labor disputes such as strikes, severe weather such as snowstorms or tornados, or such as a fire. In those cases, a contractor is entitled to a day-for-day (one day for each day of delay) adjustment in the performance schedule to account for the delay. To be considered excusable, though, the delay must truly have been beyond the contractor's control.

Another type of excusable delay is government-caused delay. For instance, virtually all contracts will include the clause at FAR 52.242-15, "Stop-Work Order." This clause gives the government the right to suspend contract performance for a period of up to ninety days (or longer, but only with the contractor's agreement). In many cases the government will direct the contractor to stop work while it considers changes to the contract's specifications or where the government's specifications are defective and performance cannot proceed until they are corrected by the government. From time to time the government may be unsure as to whether it still needs the items being produced or the services being provided. The "Stop-Work Order" clause is designed to give the government time to decide whether to allow the contract to proceed or terminate it for convenience. At the end of the ninety days the contracting officer must either rescind the order or terminate the contract.

In situations where the government has stopped the work under the contract, a contractor is entitled to an additional day of performance time for each day it was stopped. In addition, the contractor could be entitled to an adjustment in the contract price. The concept is called "unabsorbed overhead," and it is meant to reimburse the contractor for certain expenses that it continues to incur when its facilities are idled due to action or inaction on the part of the government. If a contractor wants an adjustment in the contract performance schedule or price, the clause requires that the contractor assert its right to an adjustment within thirty days after the conclusion of the stop-work period. Remember, though, that any price adjustment sought will be subject to the same negotiation rules (i.e., the Truth in Negotiations Act) as an adjustment as a result of changes.

There are also situations that may arise where performance is delayed by government action or inaction that is not associated with a formal stop-work order. Contractors may find themselves delayed by defective government specifications, but the contracting officer elects not to officially stop the work while the specifications are being corrected. In such situations a contractor should assert its right to an adjustment in the contract's performance schedule or price as soon as possible, but certainly before final payment. When a contractor submits a request for final payment, it is generally considered a release of any claims that have not been excluded from the request.

INEXCUSABLE DELAYS

Inexcusable delays are those that are considered to be within the control of the contractor. If a subcontractor stops performing, that is considered an inexcusable delay because the prime contractor chose that subcontractor and is responsible for its performance or nonperformance. If a contractor has unforeseen increases in its performance costs and/or runs into financial problems which affect performance, these are also inexcusable delays. In the case of inexcusable delays, the government may demand that the contractor pay something in exchange for resetting the performance schedule (referred to as "consideration"). In extreme cases, the government may elect to terminate the contract for default (see below).

In some situations there can be both excusable delays, such as defective government specifications, and inexcusable delays, such as supplier problems, going on at the same time. In that event, a contractor is still entitled to an extension of the contract schedule, but it would not be entitled to an adjustment in the contract price.

If a contractor believes its contract performance will be delayed, regardless of whether it would be considered excusable or inexcusable, it is imperative that it notify the contracting officer immediately. Contractors are often reluctant to "announce" that they will not be meeting a contract's performance schedule in advance. However, if the delay is the result of some action by the government, a contractor will need to get it on the record, at the time, that it will be (or is being) delayed. While no one wants to be perceived as a constant complainer, a contractor should not wait until the next time it is bidding on a contract, and is advised that the government considers its past performance to be sub-standard, to state that the delays it experienced last year or the year before were not its fault. Even if a contractor expects to be delayed due to circumstances that would be considered inexcusable, informing the contracting officer ahead of time and explaining what steps are being taken to minimize any delay shows that the contractor is proactive and concerned with the relationship.

LIQUIDATED DAMAGES

The use of "liquidated damages" clauses is frequent in certain government contracts, such as contracts for construction or renovation projects. Liquidated damages in contract law are damages for non-performance in situations in which computing actual damages would be uncertain. The parties then agree in advance to a specified figure to compensate the non-breaching party for its damages. Liquidated damages clauses are generally used in construction-type contracts that call for completion of the work by a set date, although I have seen them used on occasion in supply contracts. Most of these clauses use a daily dollar figure as a deduction for every day completion of the project is delayed, say, $500 or $1,000 per day. In supply contracts the figure is usually described as a percentage of the value of the delayed items (1/15 of 1 percent of the value of each item for each day of delay, for example). While this may sound like some sort of fine or penalty (which it is), the government is careful to couch the figure in terms of an attempt by the parties to establish an agreed figure for the government's damages in the event the contractor is inexcusably late in completing the contract (even though it is the government that unilaterally established the rate in the solicitation). This is because penalties are illegal in contract law (government and commercial), whereas an attempt by the parties to quantify inexact damages in advance is not. There has been much litigation by contractors who have contended that the liquidated damages assessed against them amounted to an improper penalty as being out of proportion to any actual damages the government may have suffered. I know of no case where the argument was successful. Indeed, in one case our office handled a contractor producing ammunition pouches for the Army (a $20 item) that was assessed almost $700,000 in liquidated damages for late deliveries. We argued that the penalty was grossly out of proportion to any potential damages the government might have suffered. We were unsuccessful. If the solicitation on which a potential competitor intends to bid or offer has a liquidated damages clause, it should consider its approach carefully, because if it is unable to perform on time, the cost could be significant. Nor can a contractor expect any help from the contracting officer, since such liquidated damages deductions are often assessed automatically and no one is likely to undertake an effort to undo them.

TERMINATIONS FOR CONVENIENCE

There are two types of terminations: "Termination for Convenience of the Government" and "Termination for Default," and the ramifications for the contractor could not be more different.

The concept of the government's right to terminate a contract without suffering breach of contract penalties grew out of the government's need to cancel war-time contracts once the war ends. Thus there was created the "Termination for Convenience of the Government" clause, which allows the government to cancel any contract for almost any reason. That clause is considered so basic to government contracting that it is considered to be part of a contract even if it had been inadvertently omitted (under the Christian doctrine). In theory, the purpose of the clause is to account for changed circumstances, but there are very few limits on the government's right to terminate a contract for convenience. About the only requirement is that the decision be taken in good faith and not be for the purpose of simply getting out of a contract because of the discovery of a better bargain somewhere else.

Convenience Termination Settlements

When the government terminates a contract under the "Termination for Convenience of the Government" clause, a contractor is to be paid the contract price for any products it has completed but not shipped or any services it has provided but not yet billed. A terminated contractor is also entitled to be paid the costs it has incurred in performing on the terminated portion of the work. Examples of such items include acquired materials and components and labor expended on work-in-process that will not be completed. A terminated contractor is also entitled to its mark-up (overhead, G&A, and profit) on those costs. The contractor does not, however, receive the profit it would have realized had it completed performance; it only receives profit applicable to its incurred cost at the percentage it would have achieved had it been allowed to complete the contract. However, there is one proviso concerning profit: If a terminated contractor was losing money performing, the government will determine the percentage of loss the contractor was incurring and then reduce the settlement payment by that "loss factor." As with a change, a contractor cannot be made better off by a termination for convenience than it would have been had it completed the contract.

As part of the termination settlement, the government will pay for settlements with subcontractors. However, contractors do not receive profit on the amounts of those subcontractor settlements. Also, and this is well worth remembering, any legal and accounting expense incurred in preparing and negotiating the termination settlement is paid by the government as "settlement expenses."

Normally when a contract is terminated for convenience, a special contracting officer, a termination contracting officer (TCO), is appointed. The TCO's function is to negotiate the settlement with the contractor. If the contractor and the TCO cannot reach an agreement, the disputes process exists for the contractor to seek a larger recovery. I would note that if and when a contractor ceases pursuing a negotiated settlement and moves into the disputes process, the government is no longer responsible for legal and accounting expenses. Professional costs incurred in pursuing negotiations are reimbursable; costs incurred in going the disputes route are not.

Terminations for Default

In government contracting, the most drastic sanction a contract can suffer is a termination for default. The "Default" clause allows the contracting officer to act unilaterally in terminating a contract. In such a situation, usually where the contractor has been inexcusably late in performance, the contractor receives no payment other than payment for products or services accepted prior to the termination. There is no payment for finished goods not yet delivered or for costs of performance. In addition, the government has the option, if it still needs the products or services, of procuring them elsewhere. If the new prices are higher than those in the contract, the defaulted contractor is liable for the difference. These are called "reprocurement costs."

If a contract has been terminated for default and the contractor believes the action to have been unjustified, it may challenge the action by way of the disputes process. Because a default termination is such a drastic sanction, the government must be both correct in its reasons and have followed all procedural steps required prior to terminating for default. Courts have held that the fact that the government has a right to terminate a contract for default does not mean it must do so. Even in a situation where the contractor is technically in default, the decision to terminate must have been a reasonable exercise of the contracting officer's discretion in that particular situation.

The most common examples where default terminations have been overturned on appeal are those cases where the government has been found to have "waived" its right to terminate for default. A waiver arises where the contractor is late in delivery, and rather than terminating for default, the contracting officer exhorts the contractor to maximize its efforts at performance. If the contractor responds by incurring additional expense in its efforts to perform, the government may not then "pull the rug out from under" the contractor by terminating for default due to the previous lateness. In order to regain its right to terminate for default, the government must establish a new, reasonable due date for deliveries. Contractors need to bear in mind that if they abandon performance, they will lose the right to claim waiver as a defense. Although it may be in inexcusable default, a contractor must continue to make an effort to perform if it hopes to have any claim to a waiver defense in the event the government does terminate the contract for default. Be aware also, though, that the concept of waiver generally is only available in contracts for supplies. It does not work as a defense to the termination of service or construction contracts.

If a contractor is late in delivery, the government may terminate for default without any advance notice, so long as it acts promptly. However, the default clause allows the government to terminate for other reasons aside from a failure to deliver. In service contracts, for instance, a failure to have sufficient numbers of personnel on site can be a cause for a default termination. Another example might be where the government learns that the contractor's bank has withdrawn its financing. In such a case where the contracting officer proposes to terminate a contract for default for a reason other than failure to deliver, he or she must first send what is usually referred to as a "ten-day letter." That letter can be either a "cure notice," in which a contractor is given ten days to "cure" the default, or a "show cause" letter, in which a contractor is given ten days to explain why it is not in default or why the default was beyond its control. In a cure notice, the letter will list some condition that the government considers to be "endangering" contract performance and state that the contractor has ten days to remedy ("cure") the condition. A cure notice is akin to the "request for adequate assurances" allowed in the commercial world under the Uniform Commercial Code (U.C.C.). In the case of a cure notice, however, the only response the government is seeking is that the condition has been cured. A "show cause" letter, on the other hand, essentially gives a contractor the chance to explain why it is not really in default, that the problems arose through no fault of its own, and were beyond its control.

In either case a contractor must take the letter seriously and respond within the time allowed. Even where the problem is a contractor's fault, it should respond to the letter and at least explain the steps it is taking to correct the situation. A failure to respond will be treated as an admission by the contractor that it is default and has no explanation or excuse. The government will then be free to terminate the contract for default.

Should the contractor prevail in a challenge to a default termination, the termination is converted to a termination for convenience of the government, on the theory that the government could have terminated the contract for convenience in any event. The contractor then receives its compensation under the "Termination for Convenience" clause rather than as a breach of contract. The basis for that theory is that since the government could have terminated the contract for convenience in the first place, the contractor should not be in a better position because of an erroneous termination for default.

NOVATIONS AND CHANGE OF NAME AGREEMENTS

Federal law prohibits transfer or assignment of a federal contract. This is to prevent people from bidding on contracts and then shopping the contract around to the company willing to pay the highest fee. There is a way, however, that a contract can be transferred, and that process, covered in FAR 42.12, is called "Novation." Basically, when a company acquires all of a government contractor's assets, or all of the assets used in performance of a particular contract, the purchaser can request that the government recognize it as the successor contractor through the Novation process. Generally the government will go along with the request, provided it can be verified that the purchaser has the ability (technical and financial) to complete the contract and the seller agrees to be responsible for the purchaser's performance. Novation is accomplished by the signing of a three-way "Novation Agreement" in the format set forth in FAR 42.1204. A Novation is generally not necessary when the asset transfer is accomplished by way of a stock purchase, for in that case the contractor remains the same, and only the ownership changes (much like in the case of a large publicly traded company). Where the contractor merely wishes to change its name, a simple agreement in FAR 42.1205 is used to effect the change of the contractor's name.

CONCLUSION

If the three most important elements in real estate are "location," "location," and "location," then the three most important elements for you insofar as contract administration in government contracting are "authority," authority," and "authority." If you are unsure as to whether the government employee giving you directions has the authority to give those directions, you need to contact your contracting officer immediately and then document the direction you receive. After you have done the work, it is too late to seek guidance. If you have been given changed work, be sure to accurately accumulate and allocate the additional cost.

Chapter 11

CONTRACT PERFORMANCE ISSUES

Winning a government contract may often be a difficult and time-consuming process, but performing on one may prove even more difficult unless the contractor devotes the proper level of attention. There are numerous issues that will almost certainly crop up as contract performance proceeds, and some of these issues can have serious consequences for the contractor who does not know how to deal with them

BIDDING MISTAKES DISCOVERED AFTER PERFORMANCE HAS BEGUN

In Chapter 8, I discussed mistakes in bidding. However, what happens when a mistake is not discovered until after contract performance has begun? How a mistake is handled may depend on whether the mistake is bilateral (a mistake made by both parties), such as both parties being unaware at the time of bidding that ground to be excavated is saturated with discarded oil, or unilateral (meaning a mistake made by one party alone, such as failing to include the cost of a required component in the bid price). In the case of the former, the contractor will certainly be entitled to relief from contract performance. In the case of the latter, the issue is far more complicated.

If a government contractor discovers that its bid contained a mistake, and the mistake was clearly the contractor's (i.e., unilateral), its ability to obtain relief is governed by FAR 14.407-1. That provision states that a mistake in a contractor's bid not discovered until after award may be corrected, if correcting the mistake would be favorable to the government without changing the essential requirements of the specification. A contract may be "reformed" to increase the price (but not higher than the next lowest acceptable bid) where there is "clear and convincing" evidence that a mistake was made, and it is clear either that the mistake was mutual, or that the mistake was so apparent the government knew or should have known of it. As I discussed in Chapter 8, if a bidder's price was so low compared to its competitors that the government should have suspected that the bidder had made a mistake, FAR 14.407-(4) requires that the contracting officer advise the bidder of the probability of a mistake. A failure on the part of the contracting officer to alert the bidder to the possibility that it had made a mistake where it should have been apparent effectively converts a unilateral mistake into a mutual mistake and the contractor will likely be able to have the contract reformed or be excused from contract performance.

As I cautioned in Chapter 8, though, there is no relief when the mistake is simply one of poor judgment. For example, to use the oil in the ground scenario I mentioned above, suppose the presence of oil was obvious to anyone who looked, and suppose the government allowed prospective bidders access to the site for a pre-bid inspection. If a bidder submitted a bid without having visited the site first, its claim of mistake will likely not be successful.

DIFFERING SITE CONDITIONS

A common situation construction contractors confront is unforeseen sub-surface conditions that delay or increase the cost of performance. To avoid having bidders include a contingency factor in their prices to protect against such situations, the clause at FAR 56.236-2, "Differing Site Conditions," is mandatory for inclusion in all solicitations for fixed-price construction contracts. To qualify as a "differing site condition," the condition had to be in existence at the time the contract was awarded. The mere fact that neither the drawings nor specifications mentioned the condition does not automatically qualify it as a differing site condition.

Under this clause the contractor is required to notify the contracting agency of any subsurface or latent physical conditions on-site that differ materially from those indicated in the contract, or unknown physical conditions on-site that are of an unusual nature, meaning they differ materially from those ordinarily encountered and generally recognized as inherent in the type of work provided for in the contract. The contracting agency is then required to investigate, and if the condition is confirmed, make an equitable adjustment in the contract price as well as the time for performance.

The companion clause to the "Differing Site Conditions" clause is the clause at FAR 52.236-3, "Site Investigation and Conditions Affecting the Work." Under the terms of this clause, also mandatory for inclusion in solicitations for fixed-price construction contracts, by submitting a bid the bidder acknowledges that it took all the steps reasonably necessary to ascertain the nature and location of the work, and that it investigated and satisfied itself as to any general and local conditions that could affect the work or its cost. The clause specifically references "the character, quality, and quantity of surface and subsurface materials or obstacles to be encountered insofar as this information is reasonably ascertainable from an inspection of the site, including all exploratory work done by the government." In other words, a subsequent claim of a differing site condition will not get very far if the condition was one that a reasonable investigation would have disclosed and the contractor had failed to undertake that investigation before submitting its bid.

SUPPLYING FOREIGN PRODUCTS

There are a number of laws that regulate the sale of foreign-made products to the government. These laws create an often-confusing patchwork of overlapping requirements and contractors will need to be aware of what can and cannot be sold to the government. For example, the same foreign product that contractors are permitted to supply as a component of a larger system may be unacceptable when it is purchased as a stand-alone item.

Several years ago our office was retained by a firm that had contracted to supply aluminum roasting pans to the GSA. The roasting pan is a component of the field kitchen used by crews fighting forest fires. The contractor who supplied the complete field kitchen procured the roasting pans from a company in China, which was perfectly permissible since the roasting pan is only a component of the end item (the field kitchen) and amounts to only a small fraction of the total cost. My client bid on the contract to supply some fifty thousand replacement roasting pans and ordered them from the same company in China that had supplied them to the contractor producing the field kitchen. However, the GSA rejected the roasting pans and ultimately terminated the contract for default. The reason: under the contract the contractor could not supply foreign (i.e., Chinese) roasting pans as an end product, even though the exact same roasting pans were acceptable as a component of the complete field kitchen supplied by the previous contractor.

The Buy American Act

The Buy American Act is the basic law covering foreign products. It is applicable to every contract to which the government is a party. There are two requirements for an item to qualify for sale to the government under the Buy American Act. First, the end product must be produced in the United States, and second, at least 50 percent of the cost of manufacturing the product must be incurred in the United States. As can readily be seen, the Buy American Act does not require that an item be 100 percent American. The contractor can use foreign materials, for instance, so long as those materials make up less than 50 percent of the cost of the item, and the end product is manufactured in the United States. For example, in one case a contractor imported watch movements from Switzerland and assembled them in the U.S. Virgin Islands, adding an American watchband. Because the work done in the Virgin Islands amounted to more than 50 percent of the manufacturing cost, and because the U.S. Virgin Islands is considered part of America, the watches met the requirements of the Buy America Act and could be supplied to the government. A contractor can even utilize some foreign labor in producing the end product, provided any manufacturing done outside of the United States does not proceed to the point where there is an identifiable end product, for then the end product would not be considered to have been manufactured in the United States. Minor assembly, cleaning, and packaging of an imported item in the United States, for example, does not make that item American.

In reviewing a solicitation, a potential bidder is likely to run across clauses that refer to "performed in the United States" or "manufactured in the United States." Unless stated otherwise in a specific clause, the term "United States" includes all fifty states, together with outlying territories, such as Puerto Rico, the U.S. Virgin Islands, and Guam.

Appropriations Act Restrictions

In addition to the Buy American Act, there are also statutes that operate to restrict how Congressionally-appropriated funds are spent. The best known of these is the Berry Amendment, named for a Congressman in the 1940s who first proposed it. Originally an annual enactment as part of appropriations for the Department of Defense (DOD), it is now a "stand-alone" statute. The Berry Amendment restricts DOD from using appropriated funds to purchase any item of clothing or textiles that is not "wholly" produced in the U.S. In this instance, "wholly" means just that: an item covered by the Berry Amendment may not have any foreign content whatsoever. Even the thread that is used to sew a garment together must be American. The Berry Amendment is incorporated into solicitations by the use of a DFAR clause 252.225-7012, "Preference for Certain Domestic Commodities." The clause prohibits a contractor from supplying any of the following items if there is any foreign material or labor in them:

- Food

- Clothing and the materials and components thereof (including any item of clothing)

- Tents and the structural components thereof

- Cotton and other natural fiber products

- Spun silk yarn for cartridge cloth

- Synthetic fabric and coated synthetic fabric, including all the fibers thereof

- Canvas products

- Wool, in any form including clothing

- Any item of individual equipment containing or manufactured from fibers, yarns, fabrics, or materials listed above

There are several exceptions, most notably for products or materials where the government has determined there is not sufficient quality and quantity available in the United States. These are called Domestic Non-Availability Determinations (DNADs) and are maintained on a Defense Department website. There are also other exceptions, including purchases made in combat zones overseas.

A similar restriction applies to purchases of clothing and textiles by the Department of Homeland Security. It is usually referred to as the Kissel Amendment after a former Congressman from North Carolina. There is, however, one major difference between "Berry" and "Kissel." While Berry represents an absolute prohibition with no exceptions, Kissel includes an exception for obligations under international agreements, such as NAFTA or the Trade Agreements Act. The reason Berry does not have such exceptions, presumably, is that it predates virtually all free trade agreements whereas Kissel, enacted within the past ten years, came after most of them had already been in place.

Contractors are often confused as to which requirement governs when a solicitation contains both the Buy American Act FAR clause and the Preference for Certain Domestic Commodities DFAR clause. A good rule of thumb in this and similar situations is that the more stringent requirement is generally the one that governs.

Other prohibitions on supplying foreign products under DOD contracts include (but are not limited to): munitions manufactured by a Chinese company (DFAR 252.225-7007); specialty metals not smelted in the United States, including steel, nickel and iron-nickel alloys, cobalt alloys, titanium and titanium alloys, zirconium and zirconium alloys (DFAR 252.225-7008); articles containing specialty metals (DFAR 252.225-7009); supercomputers (DFAR 252.225-7011); hand or measuring tools not produced in the United States (DFAR 252.225-7015); ball and roller bearings not produced in the U.S. (DFAR 252.225-7016).

It is important to bear in mind that restrictions such as Berry and Kissel are tied to funds appropriated by Congress. If a contractor is selling to the Navy Commissary or the Army and Air Force Exchange Services for example, restrictions such as the Berry Amendment do not apply to such sales, since those organizations do not receive funding appropriated by Congress; they generate their own operating funds through their sales. Unless there is some restriction contained in the contract, a contractor is generally free to deliver a wholly foreign-made product.

Free Trade Agreements

In addition to the various statutes governing the supply of foreign products, there are various international agreements the United States has signed which override laws granting preference to domestic products. The two most prominent of these agreements are the North American Free Trade Agreement (NAFTA) and the Trade Agreement Act of 1979 (TAA), implementing the (international) General Agreement on Tariffs and Trade. NAFTA and the TAA override the Buy American Act and the Kissel Agreement, but not the Berry Amendment.

If the clause at FAR 52.225-5, "Trade Agreements," is in a solicitation (as they usually are for non-DOD solicitations), a contractor can supply an end product from any "Designated Country" just as if it were made in America. The clause is to be included in solicitations for supply and service contracts that are expected to exceed $201,000 and construction contracts that are expected to exceed $7.7 million. Designated countries include:

- WTO Government Procurement Agreement Countries

- Free Trade Agreement Countries

- Least Developed Countries

- Caribbean Basin Countries

As of February 2014 there are 122 "Designated Countries." A complete list of designated countries can be found at FAR § 25.003. Be aware, though, that there are a few oddities: while Hong Kong is a designated country under the Trade Agreements clause, China is not. Products produced in Hong Kong are acceptable for delivery under a contract including the clause (even though Hong Kong is technically a part of China); products produced in Mainland China are not.

The federal government also maintains a list of foreign countries from whom a contractor cannot purchase supplies or services for ultimate delivery to the government. Countries on the list may change from time to time, so a contractor considering acquiring some component for use in performing a government contract from overseas would be wise to check whether purchases from that prospective source are allowed. The up-to-date list is maintained at FAR Subpart 25.4, "Prohibited Sources."

DOING BUSINESS OVERSEAS

While not really related to performance on a federal contract, contractors supplying military-related products or services to the federal government will often receive inquiries from buyers overseas who have interest in their products. As might be expected, products produced for the U.S. military are highly valued by militaries throughout the world. When such an opportunity presents itself, contractors will want to be familiar with the basic U.S. laws and regulations with which they must comply.

International Traffic in Arms Regulations (ITAR)

ITAR is the common acronym for the International Traffic in Arms Regulations. ITAR is meant to implement the Arms Export Controls Act, by restricting the sale to non-U.S. persons of items on the United States Munitions List (USML). Before a contractor (or anyone else for that matter) can sell an item on the USML it must procure an export license from the Department of State (DOS). Do not be misled into a false sense of security by the use of the term "munitions." The

USML includes technology, certain types of services, and space-related items. It would be wise to check the USML to see whether an item or service is included when dealing with an inquiry from an agent for a foreign government. For more information, go to DOS's website at www.pmddtc.stste.gov.

Export Administration Regulations

The Export Administration Regulations (EAR) are issued by the United States Department of Commerce, Bureau of Industry & Security (BIS) pursuant to Congressional enactments governing the control of certain exports, re-exports, and activities. In addition, the EARs implement anti-boycott laws designed to prohibit conduct by United States persons having the effect of furthering or supporting boycotts imposed by a country against a country friendly to the United States. The export control provisions of the EARs are intended to serve the national security, foreign policy, and nonproliferation interests of the United Staes, as well as carry out its international obligations. Some controls are designed to restrict access to dual use items by countries or persons that might apply such items to uses contrary to U.S. interests. The EARs also include some export controls to protect the United States from the adverse impact of unrestricted export of commodities that are in short supply domestically. For more information, go to the BIS website at www.bis.doc.gov.

The Foreign Corrupt Practices Act

A government contractor that gets an opportunity to sell its product or services overseas will need to be mindful of the

Foreign Corrupt Practices Act. This statute makes it a criminal offense for a U.S. person ("person" includes corporations) to make a payment to a foreign official for the purpose of obtaining or retaining business. In other words, making a payment that might be considered a part of doing business in a foreign country could be considered a crime back home. The definition of foreign official is extremely broad, so a contractor should simply not get involved in this type of activity.

STATE AND LOCAL TAXATION AND REGULATION

Sales to and leases with the federal government are generally immune from state and local taxes (sales taxes, for example). That does not necessarily mean a contractor does not have to pay state or local sales taxes on articles it purchases for use on its government contract. There is a federal exemption from state or local sales taxes that would extend from the federal government to cover a contractor or a subcontractor of a prime contractor. Availability of the exemption may depend on the sales tax laws in the particular state or municipality. Specific situations will require consultation with an attorney familiar with the applicable regulations.

An interesting situation arises when government-owned property (such as Government Furnished Material or property to which the government has acquired title through operation of the Progress Payment clause) is in the possession of a contractor on the date for assessment state taxes on inventory. Contractors will need to work with their contracting officers and contracting agency counsel to determine how to deal with such a situation, as the property may be exempt from such taxation.

Another situation to keep in mind involves state price regulations for certain products. For example, some state laws provide for minimum wholesale and retail prices for milk and certain other dairy products. For a contract to supply milk to a military base mess hall or commissary, the contractor's sales are not covered by such state minimum price regulations.

Patents and Copyrights

The rules regarding patent and copyright infringement by government contractors are unique but nevertheless confusing.

With a few exceptions, every government contract includes the clause at FAR 52.227-1, "Authorization and Consent." The exceptions are simplified acquisitions in which use of the clause is optional and contracts where both performance and delivery are outside of the United States, in which case use of the clause is prohibited. The "Authorization and Consent" clause authorizes the contractor to infringe on any U.S. patent or copyright in performing under the contract. It then provides that any claim of patent or copyright infringement by the owner of that patent or copyright must be brought against the United States in the Court of Federal Claims.

There is a companion clause, FAR 52.227-2, "Notice and Assistance Regarding Patent and Copyright Infringement" that is included in every contract that includes FAR 52.227-1. This clause requires that in the event the contractor learns of a potential claim of infringement it is to notify the government and assist the government in defending the suit. Likewise, if an infringement suit is filed against the government, the contractor is required to assist in defense of the suit.

All of the above certainly sounds great. There is a third patent-related clause of which contractors need to be aware, however. It is FAR 52.227-3, "Patent Indemnity." This clause provides that in a case where a suit is brought against the government by someone alleging that a government contractor has infringed on their patent or copyright and the government loses the infringement suit, the contractor is responsible for repaying ("indemnifying") the government the amount of the judgment awarded in the suit. Bear in mind that the indemnity clause is not mandatory for inclusion in all solicitations. If it is not included, the contractor can infringe on a patent or copyright without fear of being subject to damages. The indemnity clause is mandatory, however, for all solicitations for commercial items, unless Simplified Acquisition Procedures are used in the procurement or unless both performance and delivery under the contract are to be outside of the United States. An alternate to the indemnity clause is to be used when the items being procured are not commercial items. The alternate clause provides for the contracting officer to fill in a blank, listing which of the items being procured that are not subject to the patent indemnity.

There is one other "trick" of which contractors should be aware, and it can be a real "gotcha." In most solicitations, the three clauses 52.227-1, 52.227-2, and 52.227-3 are incorporated by reference, meaning they are listed among the clauses that can be incorporated into the solicitation by means of placing an "x" in a block rather than printing out the clause in full. When reviewing a solicitation, a potential offeror may see that the first two clauses (FAR 52.227-1 and FAR 52.227-2) are checked, but the indemnity clause (FAR 52.227-3) is not (they are usually listed right after one another on the same page). Before breathing a sigh of relief, the offeror needs to look for one more patent-related clause. Solicitations for commercial items generally will incorporate the clause at FAR 52.212-4, "Contract Terms and Conditions—Commercial Items." That clause includes paragraph (b), entitled "Patent Indemnity," which contains the same indemnification requirement as the clause at 52.227-3.

PROTECTING A CONTRACTOR'S RIGHTS IN DATA

Many government contracts require the contractor to produce various data, or software or reports. While the contractor may have to give up its intellectual property rights to the government, it can protect its rights against non-government users. The basic clause is FAR 52.227-14, "Rights in Data— General." That clause, in (c), allows the contractor, without prior approval from the contracting officer, to assert copyright in scientific and technical articles "based on or containing data first produced in performance of this contract," and "published in academic, technical, or professional journals, symposia proceedings, or similar works." For all other data first produced in performance of the contract, though, prior approval of the contracting officer is required before the contractor can assert copyright. The scope of the government's rights is described in FAR 27.404-3(a)(4) as a "paid-up nonexclusive, irrevocable, worldwide license to reproduce, prepare derivative works, distribute to the public, perform publicly, and display publicly . . . for all data (other than computer software)" produced in performance of the contract. For computer software, the government gets all of the same rights, except the right to distribute the software to the public. The effect of the FAR guidance is to leave the contractor who is allowed to obtain copyright protection, with the commercial rights.

There are two (2) DFAR clauses regarding rights in data produced under DOD contracts. They are: DFAR 252.227-7013, "Rights in Technical Data—Noncommercial Items" and DFAR 252.227-7014, "Rights in Noncommercial Computer Software and Noncommercial Computer Software Documentation." These clauses give the contractor the complete right to copyright technical data and computer software. This is accomplished by allowing the contractor to place a copyright notice on any such data. However, these clauses give the government unlimited rights on data that are produced in performance under the contract. Essentially, the government gets unlimited rights by virtue of having paid for the work.

THE CONTRACTOR PERFORMANCE ASSESSMENT REPORTING SYSTEM

In performing on a federal contract, a contractor will need to be familiar with the Contractor Performance Assessment Reporting System (CPARS). The CPARS is a web-based system used by contracting officers to input data on contractor performance. Once the data is input to the CPARS system, it is then uploaded to the Past Performance Information Retrieval System database and is made available for use by agency procurement personnel in future source selections. The CPARS are intended as an aid in awarding contracts to contractors that consistently provide quality, on-time products and services that conform to contractual requirements. During the source selection process, agencies are required to notify a contractor of relevant past performance data derived from their CPARS that require clarification or could lead to a negative rating. The contractor will have access to the information about its performance posted to CPARS and have the opportunity to add its own input, as a sort of rebuttal opportunity. Obviously, it makes good sense for contractors to monitor CPARS postings about their performance, as those postings may come back to bite them in future competitions.

VALUE ENGINEERING

In the course of performing on a government contract, a contractor may find that it knows a better or more economic way of satisfying the government's needs than that laid-out in the contract specifications. It is for that reason that the FAR includes the Value Engineering (VE) Program in Part 48. Under the VE program, the contractor submits its idea by way of what is commonly referred to as a Value Engineering Change Proposal (VECP) to the contracting agency. If after evaluation the idea is accepted, the contractor and the government will negotiate an appropriate figure representing the cost savings associated with the VECP. Then, once the VECP idea is incorporated into the government specifications, the contractor receives a royalty of anywhere from 50 percent to 75 percent of that agreed cost savings beginning with the first item delivered to the government reflecting the change (under the original contract or any concurrent or subsequent contract where the changed item is to be delivered) and continuing for a period of thirty-six to sixty months, depending on the individual agency's VE Program. Alternatively, the contractor and the contracting officer can negotiate a lump-sum payment at the time the VECP is accepted based on the anticipated contracts that will include the change over the following thirty-six months.

The VE Program also allows for contractors performing on construction contracts to propose alternate methods for performing the work. In such a case, the contractor can also share in the savings, although generally only on its own contract (obviously, since each construction project is unique). If the contract is a fixed-price contract, the contractor receives 55 percent of the agreed cost savings. In the case of a cost reimbursement type contract, the contractor would receive 25 percent of the savings.

Conclusion

As I have suggested previously and as you have probably surmised by now, securing the contract may be the easy part. Performing often requires finding your way through a maze of often confusing and occasionally conflicting regulations and clauses. That is where a knowledgeable and experienced attorney can help. Most importantly, you cannot be a "hands-off" manager; your money is what is at risk.

Chapter 12

GETTING PAID

s with any other large organization, there will be times when invoices are mishandled and payments delayed. However, a contractor can minimize the frequency of those instances. When submitting an invoice to the government, the contract's billing instructions must be followed to the letter. There is nothing worse than an incorrect invoice. An invoice may not be officially rejected and returned, so it is possible that a contractor will never learn why it is not getting paid. What is worse, a replacement invoice is liable to be rejected because the payment office's records will show that the invoice had already been submitted, even though it was never paid.

There is one important fact to keep in mind when submitting an invoice. Signing that invoice represents a certification by the contractor that it has complied with all of the contract's requirements, and not just those relating to the products being delivered with that invoice. Several years ago, a photographer had a contract to be the official photographer at a military base in the mid-western United States. The contract required particular methods for disposing of the photography lab chemicals. The government discovered the photographer had dumped his chemicals down the drain in his sink. He was hit with a civil fraud claim, having certified compliance with all the contract's requirements when he submitted his invoices. As a result his right to payment was forfeited.

INVOICING UNDER FIRM, FIXED-PRICE CONTRACTS

One situation a contractor should avoid if it does not want payment issues is over-shipping a line item. Most government supply contracts are broken down into line items. For example, a government contract for screws may have as many as twenty different sizes, and each size has a separate National Stock Number (NSN) and each is a separate line-item with its own identified quantity (although most supply contracts allow for a certain percentage (+ or -) variation in quantity). Funds are allocated by line item, so once the requisite number of that particular size has been delivered, there can be no further payments against that line item. A contractor may deliver the proper total number of screws, but if it over-ships some line items and under-ships others, it will not receive payment for any of the "over-shipments." What is worse is that the government is not obligated to return the over-shipped quantities. In some cases a kind contracting officer might be convinced to adjust the line-item quantities retroactively via a contract modification, thereby allowing a contractor to get paid for the over-shipped quantities. If the contracting officer cannot be convinced to help it out by way of a modification to the line-item quantities, the contractor will have donated the excess quantities to the government.

Assuming an invoice has been prepared and submitted properly, what happens if payment is still not received? If there is no payment a contractor may be forced to go the disputes route (see Chapter 13). If, on the other hand, payment is simply late, a contractor has rights under the Prompt Payment Act. That Act provides that when the government is late with a payment it must automatically add interest for each day the payment is late. It is at the Treasury rate then in effect and it is only simple interest. It is, however, interest. What if the government fails to pay the interest automatically? If the contractor does not receive the late payment interest due within ten days of the date it received the payment, it may submit a demand for the interest. If a contractor is forced to request the late payment interest, the government owes a double interest penalty (minimum $25, maximum $5,000).

Invoicing under Cost Reimbursement Type Contracts

Cost reimbursement type contracts will include the clause at FAR 52.216-7, "Allowable Cost and Payment." This clause allows the contractor to bill its "allowable" and "allocable" costs of performance as they are incurred, generally once a month. "Allowable" refers to the rules regarding costs that can be billed to the government laid out in FAR

Part 31. Costs that may be legal and even tax deductible, such as entertainment costs, may be "unallowable" either as direct charges to the government or as part of overhead and G&A rates. Another good example is executive compensation. FAR 31.205-6(p)(1) provides for limits on the allowability of compensation for certain "senior executives." The limits on such compensation are established and revised from time to time by the Office of Federal Procurement Policy. These rules do not in any way limit what a company owner can pay himself or herself. They merely limit the amount that the contractor can submit for reimbursement by the government.

"Allocability" on the other had refers generally to direct costs, such labor or materials. In order to be billed to the government under a particular contract, those costs must have been incurred in connection with the performance of that contract. They must have been allocable to that contract from an accounting standpoint. One caveat contractors should keep in mind: the costs incurred in preparing a proposal and competing for a government contract can never be billed to the government. They are neither "allowable" nor "allocable," even to the contract that was won as a result of incurring the cost.

Under the "Allowable Cost and Payment" clause procedures, a contractor bills its indirect expenses (overhead and G&A) at projected rates established at the beginning of the applicable performance period (in a multi-year contract it would be for each year). Then, at the end of the performance period, the contractor determines if its actual rates for the period were higher or lower than the projected rates used for billing. Regardless of whether the actual rates were higher or lower, the contractor is required to submit a proposal for reconciling the actual rates experienced with the projected rates used for billing. That reconciliation will show whether the projected rates resulted in over- or under-billing of indirect expense. Once the government audits the proposal, there is to be a contract adjustment, either up or down, in the reconciliation amount confirmed by the audit.

LIMITATION OF COST/LIMITATION OF FUNDS

If a contract is of the cost reimbursement type (CPFF or CPAF), there are strict limits the contractor needs to observe in invoicing its costs. Such contracts will include the clauses at FAR 52.222-20 (Limitation of Cost) and 52.222-22 (Limitation of Funds). The Limitation of Cost clause states that the contractor and the government agree that performance of the work listed in the contract schedule will not cost the government more than the cost figure set in that schedule (excluding any fee), and that the contractor will use its best efforts to ensure that will be the case. If during performance it becomes clear that the cost of the work will exceed the amount set in the schedule, there are strict reporting requirements if the contractor expects to be paid for the services it is providing. If a contractor believes that within the next sixty days the costs it will incur, when added to the cost already incurred, will exceed 75 percent of the cost in the contract schedule, or that the total cost of performance once the contract is completed will be greater than or less than the cost in the contract schedule, it must notify the contracting officer in writing. The notice must also include a revised cost estimate. Unless the contracting officer (and not anyone else) responds in writing that the estimated costs in the contract's performance schedule have been increased, the government is not obligated to pay for services provided in excess of the amount in the performance schedule, and the contractor is not obligated to continue working.

The Limitation of Funds clause operates slightly differently, but goes to the same issues. In most cost reimbursement contracts, the government funds the work incrementally. By that I mean funding is added to the contract as previous funding is exhausted. That way the government does not have money tied up in advance of when it is needed. This clause, like the "Limitation of Cost" clause, states that the contractor and the government have agreed that the work will not cost more than the estimate in the schedule. However, it also has a notice requirement. In this case the contracting officer is to be notified, in writing, if a contractor believes that within the next sixty days the costs it will incur will exceed 75 percent of the funding previously allocated to the contract. The contractor is also required to provide the contracting officer with an estimate of the funding necessary to continue performance to completion. Also, sixty days prior to completion the contractor is required to notify the contracting officer in writing of the amount of funding necessary to complete performance. Unless the contracting officer (and no one else) notifies the contractor in writing that additional funding has been allocated to the contract, the government is not obligated to pay for work in excess of the allocated funding and the contractor is not obligated to continue working.

In the case of both of these clauses, contractors often continue providing services in the belief that the government will revise the schedule's cost estimate and/or allocate additional funding. That is known as working "at risk." If the contracting officer does come through with additional funding after a contractor provided services at risk, then its invoices will be paid. If not, the contractor will not be paid unless it can point to some action by the contracting officer that could be interpreted as encouragement to continue. The fact that the contracting officer knows a contractor is working "at risk" is not enough. Silence is not encouragement. I cannot stress this enough, and perhaps an example will drive home the point. Several years ago our office was retained by a small firm that had an info technology contract with the State Department that was incrementally funded. The contractor had exceeded the funding limit by about $600,000 worth of services it had provided. The Contracting Officer"s Representative knew the contractor was working at risk, as, apparently, did the contracting officer. However, the additional funding was never added and the contractor was unable to point to any specific action by the contracting officer that rose to the level of encouragement. We were unable to recover the money from the government.

TASK OR WORK ORDER LIMITATIONS

There is one other point worth mentioning. Cost type contracts often assign work by several different "Task Orders" or "Work Orders." For purposes of the Limitation of Cost and Limitations of Funds clauses, each task or work order is treated as a separate contract. Therefore the fact that there is funding available on one task or work order does not mean a contractor can exceed the funding available on another.

Another thing to bear in mind relates to the "Allowable Cost and Payment" clause and the reconciliation I discussed above. If the audit of a reconciliation proposal determines that the government owes the contractor money, and it has reached the limit in contract funding it will not be paid the amount due. Therefore, it behooves contractors working under contracts with this clause to get their reconciliation proposals in to the government as soon as possible after the close of each performance period, while there is a good chance that funding still can be added to the contract. For example, in the case of a five-year contract, get the reconciliation proposal for year one in as early as possible in year two. That way there will likely be funding available to pay the amount due as a result of the adjustment, and the government will then add additional funds to continue performance as the year goes on.

GOVERNMENT METHODS OF CONTRACT FINANCING—PROGRESS PAYMENTS AND ADVANCE PAYMENTS

In some cases, mainly in construction, but on rare occasions in supply contracts, the contract will provide for progress payments or advance payments. In construction contracts, progress payments are available as the work proceeds. Contractors are generally allowed to submit a request each month for payment up to the percentage of completion of the total project. The government will, of course, hold back a "retainage" percentage of each payment to cover any necessary repairs that may be required during the final inspection.

In supply contracts, the progress payments are generally made available where there will be a significant outlay of capital for materials before the contractor can begin to generate income from deliveries. Progress payments are paid as a percentage of "incurred" costs, usually 85 percent. In such situations, the standard progress payment clause provides that by making progress payments to the contractor, the government gets "title" to all materials acquired by or produced by the contractor in performing on the contract. In other words, if a contractor receives progress payments, the government gets ownership of not only the raw materials that were purchased with the progress payment money, but all work in process, all finished products, and everything else on which title could pass. In this instance, though, "title' is something of a misnomer. For instance, risk of loss for the goods remains with the contractor. In the event the materials are destroyed by a fire or flood, the government can disavow its "title" and demand its progress payments back. Insurance on inventory is, therefore, even more of a must when progress payments are involved.

The government gets repayment of its progress payment by "recouping" the same percentage of each of invoice as the percentage rate that progress payment were paid. For example, if the contractor's progress payment rate is 85 percent of incurred cost, the contractor submits its request, generally monthly, listing all of its incurred costs (including indirect expense, but not profit). The government then pays the contractor 85 percent of the cost total. When the contractor then ships product and invoices for that product, the government will deduct 85 percent of the amount of each that invoice to recoup its progress payments. Once all progress payments have been recouped, then the contractor receives payment in full on each invoice.

One major advantage granted to small businesses under the progress payment clause is that they can request progress payments based on costs that have been incurred even if not yet paid. While a large business must pay an invoice before requesting a progress payment based on that invoice, a small business can submit the invoice as part of a progress payment request, and receive the progress payment before paying the invoice. The idea is to assist small businesses in financing contract performance.

Progress payments are subject to audit. Each request will be audited (even though the funds may have already been paid). The purpose is to assure the government that a contractor's costs are running at a reasonable rate for purpose of contract completion. If an audit discloses that costs are running too high, the contract could be declared in a "loss" position. In that event, regular progress payments will be reduced by the percentage deemed to be the loss percentage.

Advance payments are covered in FAR 32.4. As the least favored method of contract financing, the FAR admonishes contracting officers to use advance payments "sparingly." Types of situations in which advance payments may be made available are:

a. Contracts for experimental, research, or development work with nonprofit educational or research institutions

b. Contracts solely for the management and operation of government-owned plants

c. Contracts for acquisition, at cost, of property for government ownership

d. Contracts of such a highly classified nature that the agency considers it undesirable for national security to permit assignment of claims under the contract

e. Contracts entered into with financially weak contractors whose technical ability is considered essential to the agency

f. Contracts for which a loan by a private financial institution is not practicable, whether or not a loan guarantee; for example, if—
   1. Financing institutions will not assume a reasonable portion of the risk under a guaranteed loan
   2. Loans with reasonable interest rates or finance charges are not available to the contractor
   3. Contracts involve operations so remote from a financial institution that the institution could not be expected to suitably administer a guaranteed loan.

g. Contracts with small business concerns, under circumstances that make advance payments appropriate

h. Contracts under which exceptional circumstances make advance payments the most advantageous contract financing method for both the government and the contractor

Where the government agrees to make advance payments available, the contracting officer is required to enter into an appropriate guarantee agreement or other form of security to protect the government's money.

GOVERNMENT FURNISHED MATERIAL

In the case of some supply contracts, the government will supply the basic material to be used by the contractor in producing the end products. This is referred to as "Government Furnished Material" or "GFM." In addition to operating as a manner of contract performance financing, the use of GFM is meant to equalize the ability of offerors to compete for the contract, by eliminating the advantage some offerors may have in getting a better price for materials or components.

Where GFM is to be made available, the solicitation will establish a price and an administrative usage rate for each end item. Offerors then bid or offer, in theory at least, a cost that includes only any additional materials needed to produce the end items, plus production costs, such as labor and indirect expense. During contract perfor-mance, GFM is requested as needed to perform the contract. Similar to the situation with progress payments, the government retains title to the GFM, but the risk of loss is on the contractor. When the contractor invoices for a shipment of finished products, the administrative rate for GFM in each product is deducted from the invoice amount and the balance of the contract price paid to the contractor. When contract performance is complete, the contractor and the government will enter into a GFM settlement. If more GFM was consumed than the solicitation established for each end item, the contractor will owe the government the additional money. If, on the other hand, a contractor is able to use less than the administrative usage rate in manufacturing the products, it can return the unused balance, for which the government will pay. In other words, there is an incentive for contractors to be more efficient in the use of GFM, for it can increase their profit.

Assigning the Right to Receive Payment

It is worth mentioning that while it is forbidden to assign or transfer a government contract, contractors can assign the right to receive payment. The federal Assignment of Claims Act allows for the assignment of the right to receive payments to someone else, so long as that someone else is a recognized financial institution, mainly a bank. The assignment should be in exchange for contract financing, for if it is the government may not offset a payment due the bank against a debt that the contractor may owe the government arising from a different contract.

BANKRUPTCY ISSUES

Much as nobody likes to hear the word, situations may arise that force a contractor to consider filing for bankruptcy protection. For example, if a contract is in danger of being terminated for default, filing in bankruptcy court bars the government from terminating the contract the same as it would bar a commercial customer from canceling a contract. The contractor, as debtor-in-possession, will be able to continue performing while it tries to correct the situation, and the government will have to continue to make payments in the meantime, so long as the contractor continues to perform. If the government is dead-set on terminating the contract, it will have to apply for permission from the bankruptcy court in order to do so.

What happens to a subcontractor when the prime contractor files for bankruptcy protection? The subcontractor must continue to perform its obligations; refusal could put a subcontractor in position of having breached the subcontract. Money that is due to a subcontractor for performance before the bankruptcy filing will be handled through the bankruptcy proceedings, but a subcontractor is likely to be just an unsecured creditor for payments pending at the time of the bankruptcy filing. Payments for shipments made or services rendered after the filing will likely be paid first as "post-petition" debts. Subcontractors in such a situation should immediately consult with an attorney knowledgeable in the area of bankruptcy law to ascertain their rights. In no event, of course, can a subcontractor seek payment from the government, regardless of whether the debt is pre-petition or post-petition, since a subcontractor is not in privity of contract with the government. See Chapter 5, Teaming Agreements.

Conclusion

If you consider receiving payment for the goods or services you have provided to the government important, you will remember the basics I have outlined here for getting paid. If you follow them and there is no intervening problem, such as an IRS tax lien issued against your business, you will receive payment. On occasion payment may take a while, such as when there is a government shutdown, but you will ultimately receive the money due you.

Chapter 13

DISPUTES

ne of the factors you will need to bear in mind when deciding whether to do business with the government is the "disputes" process. Unlike the commercial world, in government contracting a contractor does not have the right to file a lawsuit in the event it believes its contracting partner has breached the contract. A contractor's rights are established by the Contract Disputes Act (the CDA), FAR Subpart 33.2, and the contract's "Disputes" clause. The basis of such a limitation of rights is the concept of "Sovereign Immunity," meaning that the government can only be sued when and how it consents to be sued. Prior to enactment of the CDA in 1978, a contractor's rights were limited to whatever was set out in the "Disputes" clause that was in the contract. A contractor dissatisfied with the decision by the contracting officer was limited to an appeal before an agency board of contract appeals. Decisions by contract appeals boards were final, subject to only limited review in what was then known as the Court of Claims.

The CDA established a standard procedure that now governs most contracts between vendors and the government. The CDA only applies to Executive Branch contracts though (and not contracts for real property), so it does not cover contracts with the legislative or judicial branches of the federal government. Disputes arising under those contracts are handled under the terms of the contracts' "Disputes" clauses. Since the overwhelming majority of contracts are with agencies or departments of the Executive Branch to which the CDA applies, that is where I will focus.

CLAIMS

The CDA, as implemented by FAR Subpart 33.2, sets out a formal process for dispute resolution. The linchpin for the entire process is a "claim," either a government claim against the contractor or a contractor claim against the government. If it is a government claim against the contractor, it must be initiated by the contracting officer and no one else. Despite the passage of over thirty-five years since the enactment of the CDA, there is still much uncertainty over what constitutes a government claim and what constitutes a contractor claim. For example, if the government deducts money from an invoice as a result of a liquidated damages assessment, it would naturally seem that is a government claim. Recent court decisions dictate otherwise. In a 2-1 decision the Court of Appeals for the Federal Circuit upheld the dismissal of a contractor's challenge to the government's withholding of liquidated damages from its invoices. The panel ruled that in order to challenge the collection of liquidated damages from its invoices by arguing excusable delay, a contractor is required to submit its own CDA claim demanding the return of the money.

A contractor claim need not necessarily be a demand for money. A dispute may arise regarding contract interpretation and a contractor may find itself in the position of having to submit a non-monetary "claim" in order to resolve an interpretation dispute. One requirement that often results in unnecessary litigation is the requirement for a "dispute" as a pre-requisite to the submission of a claim. For example, a routine invoice or other routine request for payment that is not in dispute when submitted is not a claim. A Settlement Proposal submitted after a Termination for Convenience is not a claim when it is first submitted (since it is called a "Settlement Proposal"). Once the payment request is disputed by the government, either by way of rejection or by a failure to pay within the time allowed by the contract, the contractor can deem the request "in dispute" and resubmit it as a claim, requesting a "Final Decision" by the contracting officer. In essence, the process to be followed goes "request," then "dispute," and then "claim."

There is no special format for a claim. In the case of a claim for adjustment of the contract's terms (say for an excusable delay extension to the contract's delivery schedule), the contractor need only explain what it is that it wants, state that it is submitting a "claim" and request a "Final Decision" by the contracting officer. In the case of a claim for money, a simple written demand for the money as a matter of right (with some explanation, of course) will suffice. If the claim is for money, the CDA requires that it be in a "sum certain." In other words, it must state a precise dollar amount. A claim seeking "at least" or "approximately" or "not less than" a specific dollar figure is fatally defective. Indeed, there have been cases where the defect went unnoticed until well into the litigation, requiring the contractor to restart the process. A claim that properly states a firm amount initially can be adjusted upward though based on later information, so long as it is clearly the same claim. Also, a claim can be based on estimates, as is often the case when the claim is being submitted during performance of the contract. The claim should make clear that it is based on estimates, but it must still be in a "sum certain" as to the amount. Finally, a claim should state clearly that it is a claim, as opposed to an effort to open negotiations, for instance, and it must request a "Final Decision" by the contracting officer. It is that "Final Decision" which allows a contractor to proceed to the next level in the disputes process.

Certification of a Claim

If a money claim exceeds $100,000, it must be accompanied by a certification, signed by a company official with authority to bind the company contractually. The certification should be roughly as follows:

> I certify that the foregoing claim is made in good faith; that the supporting data are accurate and complete to the best of my knowledge and belief; that the amount requested accurately reflects the contract adjustment for which the contractor believes

the Government is liable; and that I am duly authorized to certify the claim on behalf of the contractor.

It cannot be stressed too strongly: the certification requirement is mandatory. A claim exceeding $100,000 that is not certified is fatally defective. While an incorrectly worded certification or one signed by the wrong company official is correctable, the complete lack of a certification is not. It makes no difference if the contracting officer has issued a "Final Decision" on a claim. If the claim should have been accompanied by a certification and it was not, that "Final Decision" cannot provide the basis for pursuing the dispute further; it counts for nothing. Much like the situation with claims that are not in a "sum certain," there have been instances where it was not discovered that the original claim lacked a required certification until after trial of the case. In such situations, the time and expense of the trial were wasted, as the lack of a certification meant the court lacked jurisdiction to hear the matter and the entire proceeding was a nullity. In some cases, the statute of limitations had expired during the litigation, and by the time the contractor went to resubmit its claim, it was too late.

There are other implications to the certification requirement that cannot be understated. By certifying a claim the contractor is saying that the amount of the claim is the amount the contractor genuinely believes it is owed. The CDA provides that if it is later determined that the contractor is unable to support any part of its claim, the contractor is "fined" the amount of the overstatement, together with the government's cost of investigation costs (audits, for example). In a recent case, a large defense contractor had a claim against the government worth about $13 million. However, the company's president wanted to "get the government's attention" and the claim was submitted (and certified) at $65 million. When the case was tried, the company's attorneys did not even attempt to prove the $65 million, pursuing only the $13 million legitimately owed. However, as a result of the false certification at the time the claim was originally submitted, the court awarded the government a judgment in the amount of $52 million.

Only a "Contractor" Can Pursue a Claim

It is important to keep in mind that only a "contractor" can pursue a claim under the CDA. This means, necessarily, that to pursue a claim against the federal government under the CDA, it is a requirement that the contract be with an agency of the federal government. A contract with a state or local government may be funded by the federal government, but that does not make the federal government a party to the contract, so there is no right to pursue a claim under the CDA.

As I discussed in the Chapter 5, "Teaming Agreements," a subcontractor can only pursue a claim against the government with the authorization and in the name of the prime contractor. A subcontractor with a claim against the federal government must submit its claim (with the certification, if required) to the prime contractor. The prime contractor must then add its own certification, again if certification is required, before submitting the' subcontractor's claim to the contracting officer. That does not mean that the prime contractor need necessarily agree with the subcontractor's claim. It is sufficient if the prime contractor certify that the subcontractor's claim is being submitted in good faith and reflects the amount that the subcontractor believes it is owed.

Time Limit for Claim Submission

Contractors should bear in mind that there is a strict time limit for submission of a claim under the CDA. A claim must be submitted within six years of when the right to submit a claim "accrues," or the claim is forever barred (and the same rule applies to a government claim). For example, if the claim is based on an unpaid invoice, the right to submit a claim accrues on the first day payment is overdue (on day thirty-one after submission, for example, if payment is due in thirty days). The claim must be submitted within six years of that day. The six-year time limit for claim submission is considered "jurisdictional," meaning no one has the power to extend it or waive it. Our office had an occasion to represent a client who had over $200,000 in unpaid invoices that had accrued over a number of years. During that period the company's accounting personnel and officials from the payment office spent considerable time and effort trying to reconcile company records with those of the payment office, including trips to the payment office. Finally, officials at the payment office said they would not participate in any further reconciliation efforts, and the company decided to pursue its "disputes" rights by submission of a claim. Unfortunately, some of the invoices were by that time more than six years old. We argued that the government's participation in efforts to resolve the unpaid invoices should have operated to extend the six-year claim submission deadline, however we were unsuccessful. The courts ultimately ruled that each invoice represents a distinct request for payment, and the right to submit a claim "accrues" on the first day payment is overdue. Once the six years elapsed for a particular invoice, a claim could no longer be submitted.

Finally, interest on a claim against the government does not begin to accrue interest until it is presented as a claim in accordance with these procedures. Once a contractor has presented a proper (meaning compliant with the requirements of the CDA and the FAR) claim, simple interest (at Treasury rates) will run on the claim until payment is made.

The Contracting Officer

The starting point for the "disputes" process is the contracting officer. If the claim is by the government, it is the contracting officer who issues it. If a contractor wants to pursue a claim, it must first submit it to the contracting officer. One quirk in the system is the fact that in some circumstances there can be more than one contracting officer and contractors need to figure out which one is the proper one for submittal of a claim. For example, there is often one contracting officer who awards the contract (the procuring contracting officer or PCO) and another whose job it is to administer the contract (the administrative contracting officer or ACO). Unless the dispute involves an area of the contract for which authority has been delegated to the ACO, claims should be submitted to the PCO. Also, in the case of a GSA Schedule contract, there will be a GSA contracting officer for the Schedule contract. However, task or delivery orders are issued by contracting officers from various agencies. If a claim requires interpretation of the Schedule contract's provisions, it goes to the GSA contracting officer; if the task or delivery order provisions are at issue, it goes to the contracting officer who issued the task or delivery order on behalf of that agency.

Once a contractor has submitted its claim to the proper contracting officer, under the CDA he or she has sixty days to issue the "Final Decision" (although the CDA prohibits the contracting officer from issuing a "Final Decision" on a claim where fraud is suspected). If the claim is so complex that it cannot be acted on in sixty days, the contracting officer must inform the contractor before the sixty-day period expires by what date the "Final Decision" will be issued. There are two basic requirements for a "Final Decision." First, it must clearly state that it is the "Final Decision" of the contracting officer. This is so that the contractor clearly understands that there has to been a decision on the claim. Any suggestion in the decision letter that the government might be willing to negotiate or consider additional information negates the decision's finality. Second, the "Final Decision" must advise the contractor of its appeal rights. Failure of the decision to contain the appeal information may prevent the deadline clocks from commencing to run.

Obligation to Continue Performance

One important consideration for contractors to keep in mind: unlike the commercial world, the standard "Disputes" clause in virtually every government contract requires a contractor to continue performing the contract while the disputes process plays out. Refusing to perform because of a dispute can have dire consequences, even if a contractor is acting in good faith and is correct in its interpretation. Not too long ago there was a reported situation in which the government purported to exercise the option in a contract. The contractor, who was losing money in performance, contended that the option exercise had been improperly effectuated and refused to continue with the work. As a result, the government terminated the contract for default. The contractor challenged the termination in court, arguing that the improper exercise of the option excused it from continuing to perform the work. The court agreed that the option had been improperly exercised. However it upheld the termination, ruling that under the contract's "Disputes" clause, the contractor had to continue performing. The court pointed out that in the event of an ineffective option exercise, the contracting officer's action is considered a "change," entitling the contractor to recovery based on its costs. Therefore, the contractor in this instance was required to continue performing while it disputed the exercise of the option and sought recovery of the cost of performing the "changed" (i.e., added) work.

Once the contracting officer issues the "Final Decision," if the contractor is dissatisfied with the decision, it may either appeal the decision to one of the agency boards of contract appeals or file suit in the Court of Federal Claims (CFC). There are strict time limits for proceeding. Appeals to a board of contract appeals must be filed within ninety days of receipt of the "Final Decision," while suits in the CFC must be filed within one year. Missing the deadline for filing with a board or the court renders the tribunal without jurisdiction to consider the claim, and no one, not the judge nor the government lawyers, have the authority to waive that jurisdictional defect. What happens if the contracting officer fails or refuses to act on a claim? In that case, once the sixty days have elapsed, the contractor is free to appeal or file suit. Under the CDA, when a contracting officer fails to issue a "Final Decision," the contractor is permitted to treat the claim as "deemed denied" by the contracting officer. There is no ninety-day or one-year deadline for appealing from a deemed denial, since there was no actual "Final Decision" by the contracting officer to start the clock running.

Agency Boards of Contract Appeals

The next level for most disputes is an "appeal" of the contracting officer's decision to one of the agency boards of contract appeals There are four such boards that together cover virtually all federal government contracts covered by the CDA: The Armed Services Board of Contract Appeals (ASBCA), for appeals involving contracts issued Department of Defense agencies, as well as contracts with the National Aeronautics and Space Administration (NASA); the Civilian Board of Contract Appeals (CBCA), with jurisdiction over contracts issued by civilian agencies; the Tennessee Valley

Authority Board of Contract Appeals (TVABCA) for disputes involving TVA contracts; and the Postal Service Board of Contract Appeals (PSBCA), for Postal Service contracts. These boards hear what are referred to as "appeals" from "Final Decisions" by the contracting officer (including "deemed denied Final Decisions"), although, as noted above, a "Final Decision" on a claim lacking a required certification cannot serve to provide jurisdiction for an appeal.

Most disputes are pursued before one of these boards because they provide a less expensive forum than the CFC. There is no filing fee and, unlike a court, a corporation can be represented by a corporate officer. Appeals are heard by Administrative Law Judges (ALJ). There is no jury. Even though the terminology used is "appeal" from the contracting officer's "Final Decision," the appeal is heard *de novo*, meaning the "Final Decision" is not accorded any weight in the appeal process. The ALJ hears the case as if the "Final Decision" was never issued. As discussed above, the time limit for filing such an appeal (ninety days) is critical; a board of contract appeals cannot waive the ninety-day time limit and cannot consider a late appeal. Convenient aspects of the contract appeals boards include offering alternate dispute resolution (ADR) and accelerated small claims procedures, such as appeals being decided "on the record," meaning the various documents in the appeal file, together with additional documents and written argument submitted by the parties. Hearings can be held where the contractor is located, even if that is outside of the U.S. Judges on the ASBCA frequently travel to Europe or the Far East to conduct hearings on contracts between military units based there and local contractors.

While there are cost and convenience considerations that make going to a board of contract appeals attractive, there are negatives to consider when electing a forum in which to pursue a claim. Appeals to the agency boards are handled by attorneys at the contracting agency. Agency attorneys have no authority to settle disputes. Only the contracting officer whose decision is at issue has the authority to settle the dispute. Obviously, that creates difficulties in trying to settle, as it will generally require the contracting officer who denied the claim in the first instance to approve the settlement. There was a case reported by the ASBCA not long ago in which the contractor and his attorney met with the contracting officer and the government attorney to negotiate settlement of a claim. At the end of the negotiations, an agreement was reached which was signed by the two attorneys. However, the contracting officer later refused to process the settlement. It seems he disagreed with the settlement, although he had never indicated so at the settlement negotiations meeting. The fact that the contracting officer was present and did not object did not serve to make the settlement agreement binding on and enforceable against the government.

A second consideration, in the event a claim is not suitable for an accelerated procedure, is time. The boards are slow in deciding cases. The average time for a decision from the ASBCA is one year after all the post-trial briefs have been filed. Part of the time interval stems from the sheer number of appeals. Additionally, the boards generally "bifurcate" appeals (dividing liability issues from damages). Liability is handled first, the idea being not to waste time hearing damages evidence until it is clear who has prevailed on liability. If a trial is required, it may take as much as two to three years to resolve who was at fault, considering pre-trial proceedings, the trial, post-trial briefing, and then the wait for a decision. If the contractor prevails in the liability phase the board will remand the matter back to the contractor and the contracting officer with instructions to attempt negotiating a damages settlement. If there is no agreement on damages, the matter goes back to the board for a second appeal on the damages issue, which may require a second trial with a second round of post-trial briefing and another two to three years.

THE COURT OF FEDERAL CLAIMS

The alternative to the boards of contract appeals is a "direct action" suit filed with the CFC, based in Washington, D.C. Unlike U.S. district court judges who are appointed for life, judges on the CFC are appointed by the President (subject to confirmation by the Senate) to fixed fifteen-year terms. In most other respects, procedures in the CFC are similar to cases tried in the U.S. district courts. It is generally the route to take for claims that are of a high dollar value. There is a filing fee and a corporation must be represented by an attorney, so the expense to the contractor is increased immediately. While the CFC does have an Alternative Disputes Resolution (ADR) Program, there is no small claims procedure. However, unlike the contract appeals boards, judges of the CFC generally do not bifurcate cases. If a trial is required, liability and damages are tried together just as in any other court proceeding. The result is a faster resolution of the dispute.

Like the boards of contract appeals, cases before the CFC are tried without a jury, and like contract appeals board proceedings, the contracting officer's "Final Decision" is not accorded any weight. Suits in the CFC are defended by the Department of Justice Civil Division in Washington, D.C. These attorneys, unlike agency attorneys in appeals to one of the contract appeals boards, have the authority to settle cases without the contracting officer's concurrence. Indeed, I have been involved in several cases over the years that were settled by Department of Justice attorneys over the objections of the contracting agency.

THE COURT OF APPEALS FOR THE FEDERAL CIRCUIT

A contractor dissatisfied with the decision by a contract appeals board or the CFC has one remaining avenue it can pursue. It can appeal to the U.S. Court of Appeals for the Federal Circuit (CAFC). This court does not conduct trials. Rather a three judge panel decides the appeal based on the record from the contract appeals board or the CFC. The panel will accept the factual findings of the lower tribunal, provided they are supported by "substantial evidence;" but conclusions of law made by the lower tribunal are ignored.

The CAFC is the last stop in virtually all CDA cases. While either party has a right to seek review by the U.S. Supreme Court (by way of a writ called *Certiorari*), the Supreme Court only accepts around 2 percent of the requests for review it receives. Generally, only cases that raise issues of major importance to a broad spectrum of the public are accepted for review.

THE EQUAL ACCESS TO JUSTICE ACT

Obviously, unless the contractor is a giant company, like a Boeing or Lockheed Martin, the government will have significant advantages in any litigation. In an effort to make things a little more equal in litigation, Congress passed the Equal Access to Justice Act (EAJA). Under EAJA contract appeal board judges and CFC judges have the authority to award legal fees to litigants who are successful against the government. The requirements are first that the applicant must be a "prevailing party," meaning it must have secured a decision in its favor by the court or board (an actual decision, not a settlement). Next, the applicant must be a small business with a net worth of no more than $7,000,000. Third, an application for an EAJA award must be submitted within thirty days after the decision in the applicant's favor is final. Finally, the judge who rendered the decision in the litigation must find that the government's litigation position was not "substantially justified." In another words, merely prevailing is not sufficient; the judge must conclude that the government adopted a litigation strategy that was not "substantially justified" either based on prevailing law or the law or the facts of the case. The judge may then award the successful litigant the legal fees it incurred in pursuing the case (at certain specified rates). If the contractor prevailed in only part of the litigation, the judge may make a partial award under EAJA.

CONCLUSION

If you are lucky, you will never have to pursue your rights under the contract's "Disputes" procedures. Knowing how those procedures work and when to invoke them, however, may help both you and the government avoid having to invoke them.

Index

Numbers

8(a) Program, 4, 55–58, 157–58

A

AbilityOne, 103–4
ACO (Administrative Contracting Officer),
vi, 159–160, 221
acquisition of commercial items, 82–84
acquisitions, simplified, 84–86
ADA (Americans with Disabilities Act), 28–29
ADA (Anti-Deficiency Act), 12, 125–26
adjustments, equitable, 162–64, 164–66
Administrative Contracting Officer. *see* ACO
Administrative Law Judges. *see* ALJ
Administrative Procedure Act. *see* APA
advance payment, 207–9
adverse action, 149–150
Affordable Care Act, 25
Age Discrimination in Employment Act, 25
ALJ (Administrative Law Judges), 224
Americans with Disabilities Act. *see* ADA
Anti-Deficiency Act. *see* ADA
Anti-Kickback Act, 38–39, 74
APA (Administrative Procedure Act), 153
Armed Services Board of Contract Appeals. *see*
ASBCA
Arms Export Controls Act, 189 ,
ASBCA (Armed Services Board of Contract
Appeals), vi, 223, 224–26
Assignment of Claims Act, 210
attorneys, vi, 31
authority
awarding contracts, 10–12
in contract performance, 12–13, 159–161

B

BAFO (Best and Final Offer). *see* FPR (Final
Proposal Revisions)
bankruptcy, 211–12
Basic Ordering Agreement. *see* BOA
benefits, 22–24
Berry amendment, 185–86, 187
Best and Final Offer (BAFO). *see* FPR (Final
Proposal Revisions)
Best Value methodology, 89–91, 99
bids
collusion, 35–36
mistakes, 135–37, 179–181
preparing, 126–28

sealed, 86–88
timeliness, 131–34
withdrawing, 134–35
BIS (Bureau of Industry & Security), 190
Blanket Purchase Agreement. *see* BPA
BOA (Basic Ordering Agreement), 117
BPA (Blanket Purchase Agreement), 85–86, 117
breastfeeding, 25
bribery, 36–37
bundling, 148–49
Bureau of Industry & Security, 190
Bush, George W., 18
Buy American Act, 183–84
buying-in, 37–38, 92

C

CAFC (Court of Appeals for the Federal
Circuit), 227–28
Cardinal Changes, 161
CBCA (Civilian Board of Contract Appeals),
vi, 223
CDA (Contract Disputes Act), vii, 213–14,
214–16
Census Bureau, 2, 3
Center for Veterans Enterprise. *see* CVE
Certificate of Competency Program. *see* COC
Program
certification of claims, 216–18
CFC (U.S. Court of Federal Claims), vii,
153–55, 223, 226–27
changes in contracts, 161–62, 162–64
Christian doctrine, 19, 121, 172
CICA (Competition in Contracting Act), vii, 17,
102, 143, 150, 161
Civil Rights Act, 28
Civilian Board of Contract Appeals. *see* CBCA
claims, 214–220
certification, 216–18
contractors only, 218–19
time limits, 219–220
clarifications, 89, 97
COC (Certificate of Competency) Program,
55, 88
Code of Business Ethics and Conduct, 42, 74
COFC (U.S. Court of Appeals for the Federal
Circuit), vii
collusion in bidding, 35–36
commercial impracticability, 108–9
commercial items, 82–84
Commercially Available Off-the-Shelf. *see*
COTS

Index

Books from Allworth Press

Allworth Press is an imprint of Skyhorse Publishing, Inc. Selected titles are listed below.

The Art of Digital Branding
by Ian Corcoran (6 x 9, 272 pages, paperback, $19.95)

Brand Thinking and Other Noble Pursuits
by Debbie Millman (6 x 9, 336 pages, paperback, $19.95)

Corporate Creativity: Developing an Innovative Organization
by Thomas Lockwood and Thomas Walton (6 x 9, 256 pages, paperback, $24.95)

Emotional Branding: The New Paradigm for Connecting Brands to People
by Marc Gobé (6 x 9, 352 pages, paperback, $19.95)

From Idea to Exit: The Entrepreneurial Journey
by Jeffrey Weber (6 x 9, 272 pages, paperback, $19.95)

Millennial Rules: How to Sell, Serve, Surprise & Stand Out in a Digital World
by T. Scott Gross (6 x 9, 208 pages, paperback, $16.95)

Peak Business Performance Under Pressure
by Bill Driscoll (6 x 9, 224 pages, paperback, $19.95)

The Pocket Small Business Owner's Guide to Building Your Business
by Kevin Devine (5 ¼ x 8 ¼, 256 pages, paperback, $14.95)

The Pocket Small Business Owner's Guide to Business Plans
by Brian Hill and Dee Power (5 ½ x 8 ¼, 224 pages, paperback, $14.95)

The Pocket Small Business Owner's Guide to Negotiating
by Kevin Devine (5 ½ x 8 ¼, 224 pages, paperback, $14.95)

The Pocket Small Business Owner's Guide to Starting Your Business on a Shoestring
by Carol Tice (5 ½ x 8 ¼, 244 pages, paperback, $14.95)

The Pocket Small Business Owner's Guide to Taxes
by Brian Germer (5 ½ x 8 ¼, 240 pages, paperback, $14.95)

Rebuilding the Brand: How Harley-Davidson Became King of the Road
by Clyde Fessler (6 x 9, 128 pages, paperback, $14.95)

To see our complete catalog or to order online, please visit *www.allworth.com*.